THE INSTITUTE SERIES : 2

REASONS FOR LIVING AND HOPING
GAUDIUM ET SPES 40 YEARS ON

The Heythrop Institute for Religion, Ethics & Public Life

PUBLISHED BY THE HEYTHROP INSTITUTE FOR
RELIGION, ETHICS & PUBLIC LIFE

Heythrop College, Kensington Square, London W8 5HQ

http//www.heythrop.ac.uk/HIREPL

First published 2006

Printed in the United Kingdom at Collier Litho Ltd, Romford

A catalogue reference for this book is available from the
British Library

ISBN 1-905566-01-8

CONTENTS

INTRODUCTION

No one could be in any doubt about the uniqueness of Vatican II, and *Gaudium et spes,* the 'Pastoral Constitution' on the Church in the modern world, is one of its most original and foundational documents. It sets out the principles of the Church's relation to the world and sketches a Christian approach to some major issues before us in the social, cultural and international arena.

Reasons for Living and Hoping was a conference organised by the department for Christian Responsibility and Citizenship (Catholic Bishops Conference of England and Wales), the Heythrop Institute for Religion, Ethics & Public Life and the Benedictine Community of Worth Abbey. While it was certainly an opportunity to mark the fortieth anniversary of *Gaudium et spes,* to re-read it and acknowledge its achievement, it was also a moment to assess it in the light of our current situation. The conference lectures collected here offer a perspective and critique of the main structure and themes of the Constitution. A second volume will consist of the shorter papers given at the seminars and workshops. Together, they aim to explore the continued relevance of *Gaudium et spes* and expand its thinking into areas that the Council could not have envisaged in 1965 but which are very much questions for 2005. As a whole they demonstrate that Vatican II, especially in its great Constitutions, still represents a resource of considerable richness which we are still in the process of appropriating.

We are particularly grateful to Cardinal Walter Kasper for opening the Conference and Cardinal Cormac Murphy O'Connor for his contribution and support. Archbishop Peter Smith chaired all the preparatory meetings and was generous with his time and advice throughout.

The major documents of the Council are not only theological works of considerable depth, they are also imbued with a contemplative vision. This is why we are particularly grateful to the Abbot and community at Worth whose hospitality and rhythm of prayer and worship provided an ideal context for allowing the spirituality of *Gaudium et spes* to be experienced and explored.

Our one regret was that places at the Conference were limited. We hope that the publication of these papers will make some of its work more available.

This Conference was supported by generous sponsorship from a number of organizations, and I would like to add a final word of gratitude to them and to Moyra Tourlamain, the executive administrator of the Institute, Andrew Cooke and Ronald Santangeli who together prepared these essays for publication.

James Hanvey SJ
Director
The Heythrop Institute for Religion, Ethics & Public Life.

THE PASTORAL CONSTITUTION
GAUDIUM ET SPES

Cardinal Walter Kasper presents an appraisal of *Gaudium et Spes* as the starting point for a new inculturation of Christianity in the modern world. He argues that, though the methodology and fundamental principles of the Constitution are still valid today, they must be seen in the light of our contemporary context and applied anew in a prophetic way.

The Fundamental Aspects of the Pastoral Constitution

The Second Vatican Council issued sixteen documents in all, including some very extensive texts: four Constitutions, nine Decrees and three Declarations. Among these, one stands out in its singularity, namely the *Pastoral Constitution on the Church in the Modern World*, *Gaudium et spes.* This distinction is due not only to the fact that the Constitution had a very difficult passage during the Council, and that it required eight drafts prior to arriving at the definitive text. Rather, it is a *unicum* principally because it represents an absolute innovation in the two thousand year history of the Councils.

There had been Constitutions, Decrees and Declarations in all the preceding Councils, and theologians well understood their respective priority and merit. But a Pastoral Constitution? The very wording is innovative. Indeed, so innovative that a long introduction was included explaining the meaning of the term and outlining its binding characteristics. The originality of the title asserts the originality of its content. Indeed, the Constitution not only expounds general principles of faith, but also addresses concrete issues in the modem world, looks at the "signs of the times", speaks of science and culture, of marriage and the family, of the social order, of work, the economy, of peace and war, even of the nuclear threat. This wide range of issues has led the Constitution to be compared ironically with Noah's Ark, where a home was found for everything that did not find a place elsewhere.

With this document on the "Church in the Modern World", the Council not only spoke to its own faithful, but to the whole human family. It not only deals with internal problems of faith and discipline, but issues relating to the world, to the concerns of modern people. This direction was not foreseen at the beginning. It was only during the first session of debate that Cardinal Suenens and Cardinal Montini proposed a dual objective, namely the themes of *Ecclesia ad intra* and *Ecclesia ad extra.*

If we want to be more precise, however, the Pastoral Constitution is not really directed *ad extra*. The title does not state "message of the Church *to* the Modern World", but "the Church *in* the Modern World". The Church does not present itself to the world as *Mater et Magistra,* but understands itself as an entity within the world, in solidarity with the world. In order to illustrate this new concept, it is sufficient to cite the well-known introduction: "The joys and the hopes, the griefs and the anxieties of the men of this age, especially those who are poor or in any way afflicted, these too are the joys and hopes, the griefs and anxieties of the followers of Christ" [GS 1].

Therefore, the real innovation is not only in the title and in many of the themes of the Constitution, but in the very way that the document tackles these: namely in an attitude of dialogue. Dialogue is one of the fundamental concepts of the Second Vatican Council and of post-Conciliar debate (cf. GS 3, 19, 21, 25, 40, 43, 56, 85, 90, 92). As described by Pope Paul VI in his first Encyclical,

Ecclesiam suam (1964), this term is understood as "dialogue within the Church, with the other Churches and Ecclesial Communities, with non-Christian religions and with the modern world".

The Pastoral Constitution does not offer moralising advice to modern people, but demonstrates its attentiveness to their aspirations and needs, seeking to share their joys and sufferings. The Constitution casts a realistic eye on some of the disturbing aspects of the contemporary world, but does not affirm in an apocalyptic tone that the world is bad, that it is the work of evil; rather, it is able to recognise also its positive aspects. In speaking of the negative features, the Constitution proves the Church capable of self-criticism, which is a necessary characteristic in any dialogue. For it does not find fault only in others, but recognises the shared responsibility of Christians, for example, in the phenomenon of modem atheism (cf. GS 19). Thus, the Council courageously anticipated the *'mea culpa'* or rather *the 'nostra culpa'* of Pope John Paul II.

The Council did not evade, but rather openly confronted modern issues. It is precisely this adaptation and implementation of faith in real life experience that is meant by the word 'pastoral', which is not simply an alternative to the term 'doctrinal'. Rather, a pastoral attitude presupposes a doctrinal foundation. Pastoral care neither can nor wants to be a substitute for doctrine nor to circumvent it; more precisely, it seeks to introduce doctrine into real situations and in so doing to stress its true value.

With this Pastoral Constitution, the Council opposes itself to secular attempts to limit the field of action and interest of the Church to merely internal questions, relegating it to the 'sacristy' so to speak. Indeed, the Church does not allow itself to be marginalised and reduced to a purely private and personal dimension, for it claims a public voice. And it does so not on behalf of its own interests, but those of all humanity. The Constitution states: "Hence the pivotal point of our total presentation will be man himself; whole and entire, body and soul, heart and conscience, mind and will" [GS 3]. The Council considers fundamental existential questions: "What is man? What is this sense of sorrow, of evil, of death, which continues to exist despite so much progress? What is the purpose of these victories, purchased at so high a cost? What can man offer to society, what can he expect from it? What follows this earthly life?" [GS 10].

The Constitution seeks to eliminate the dichotomy between faith and daily experience, a distinction it believes is one of the most mistaken and destructive interpretations of modern times (cf. GS 42). Later, in his Apostolic Letter *Evangelii nuntiandi* (1975), Pope Paul VI would state that : "The split between the Gospel and culture is without a doubt the drama of our time" (20).

In confronting this crucial issue of our time we touch upon the fundamental concern of the Pastoral Constitution: how can the Church, with its message of faith, take a position regarding the existing problems of the world? Is it possible to infer automatically from the principles of faith a response to contemporary world issues? If this were so, each individual and each specific situation would be merely a 'case in point' of a general principle. This is contrary to Christian thought, which affirms the uniqueness of each person and the uniqueness of the conscience of each. For this very reason, the Pastoral Constitution maintains that, with the exception of fundamental ethical questions, it is quite legitimate for Catholics conscientiously to take their own positions regarding contemporary issues, including political ones (cf. GS 42).

The Church does not have any doctrinal competence enabling it to formulate normative solutions to individual situations. These situations can change rapidly; we will see later that the very deliberations of the Pastoral Constitution have in part now become obsolete. At the time of the publication of the Constitution in 1965, the Cold War was at its peak. Since then, the world and our society have changed dramatically in many ways. Yet how does one behave when it is not possible to rely upon unequivocal norms? This is the fundamental problem raised by the Pastoral Constitution.

The way in which the Council confronts such basic issues is surprisingly new. Indeed, it does not turn to the principle of natural law, which by traditional consensus was recognised by all, thus constituting a bridge between believers and non-believers, as well as between the faithful of other religions. The Council seeks another way. It does not place in the foreground the so-called *preambula fidei,* the natural presuppositions of faith, but the *centrum fidei,* the message of Jesus Christ. This focus is derived from a universalistic Christology based principally on Col I: 15-20: "... for in him all things in heaven and on earth were created ... all things have been created through him and for him" (cf: Jn. 1:3; Eph. 1:3; Heb. 1:2). At the end of the introduction, the Constitution affirms schematically:

> "The Church believes that Christ, who died and was raised up for all, can through His Spirit offer man the light and the strength to measure up to his supreme destiny... She likewise holds that in her most benign Lord and Master can be found the key, the focal point, and the goal of all human history. ... Hence in the light of Christ ... the Council wishes to speak to all men in order to illuminate the mystery of man and to co-operate in

11

finding the solution to the outstanding problems of our time" [GS I0].

Such Christocentric affirmations can also be found in many other paragraphs (cf: GS 22, 32, 39, 45, 93). They were often reiterated by Pope John Paul II, commencing with his very first Encyclical *Redemptoris hominis* (1979), which opens with the words: "The Redeemer of man, Jesus Christ, is the centre of the universe and of history."

The Council pursues a dual reflection on the basis of this fundamental conviction. On the one hand, it seeks to read the "signs of the times" in the light of the Gospel (cf. GS 3 ff., 10 ff., 22, 40, 42. ff, etc.); on the other, it wants to accept the challenge they present and to question itself on them in order to achieve a greater understanding of its own evangelical message (cf. GS 40, 44, 62). We are grasping an interpretation of the world, of humanity, but also of the Gospel, which matures in its fullness in an attitude of dialogue. Indeed, we could even speak in terms of a prophetic ecclesial reality.

In order to illustrate tangibly the meaning of this conception of dialogue and prophecy, we could reflect on two specific points that are discussed amply in *Gaudium et spes,* namely the vision of the modern world and the place of man in the modern world. We will limit ourselves to these two themes, given that an exhaustive overview of the many themes of the Constitution would be impossible, not least in view of the time limitation.

The Drama of the Modern World

How does the Pastoral Constitution see the modern world? How does it evaluate the "signs of the times"? The Council observes: "Today, the human race is passing through a new stage of its history. Profound and rapid changes are spreading by degrees around the whole world." [GS 4]. In more concrete terms it affirms: "Thus, the human race has passed from a rather static concept of reality to a more dynamic, evolutionary one" [GS 5]. There emerges a crisis of growth, which renders the contemporary scene more complex and which embodies a previously unknown type of anxiety. The Council takes into account the existence of a wide range of paradoxical factors: on the one hand, greater wealth than in the past and, on the other, hunger and poverty; an increasing need for freedom juxtaposed against social and physical subjugation; mutual dependence offset by conflicting tendencies, and by racial and social tension; intensified socialisation devoid of intensified personalisation; the erosion of traditional values; religious indifference; the underlying family crisis; the demand for equal opportunities for women (cf. also GS 29 and 52 ff. on this aspect) and lastly, yet equally important, the internal division in man caused by sin (cf. GS 4, 7-10). Thus, while it does not surrender to a negative and apocalyptic view, the final and definitive draft of the Pastoral Constitution does not present a unilaterally optimistic panorama.

The Constitution speaks of the fundamental problem of modern times in a new and courageous way in two respects. Firstly, it recognises the rightful autonomy of earthly affairs (cf. GS 36, 41, 56, 76), affirming that "created things and societies themselves enjoy their own laws and values which must be gradually deciphered, put to use, and regulated by men" [GS 36]. For the Council, this recognition not only represents a challenge to contemporary man, but also reflects the reality of all created things, which "are endowed with their own stability, truth, goodness, proper laws, and order" [GS 36]. From this ensues the recognition of the legitimate autonomy of science, culture and politics; this legitimate independence needs to be distinguished from a false autonomy and from a false humanism that are merely contingent and materialist, if not anti-religious.

With these affirmations, the Constitution recognises the important claim of the Enlightenment among the legitimate yearnings of modern secularisation. In so doing, the Council closes a sad chapter in the Church's recent history. The Council refutes fundamentalism, which in seeking to deduce from the principles of faith a uniform and automatic solution to human dilemmas, has often caused totally futile and - in most cases - totally senseless conflicts with science, culture and modern politics. We could mention, for example, Galileo and Darwin, and - in a quite different way - the Pontifical State.

The recognition of the legitimate autonomy of the wide variety of experience of the modern man is fundamental for the liberty of lay people in the Church; for they are the experts in these fields of experience and they have the necessary skills for which the Gospel is the source of "light and energy", if not always the direct source of information [GS 42]. Pastors must therefore respectfully recognise the rightful liberty of the laity in the Church (*Lumen gentium* 37). A second tendency also follows this same line; that is, the promotion of human rights and the condemnation of all forms of discrimination (cf. GS 21, 26, 29, 41 ff., 59, 73, 76), which are the underlying axioms of our times. The decision of the Council to take such a stance is grounded once again in creation, in the fact that God created man in his image and likeness (cf. Gen. 1:27; GSn12) In line with its Christocentric conception, the Constitution enhances this traditional theme by affirming that the true light can only be found by man in Jesus Christ. "Christ, the final Adam, by revelation of the mystery of the Father and His love, fully reveals man to man himself and makes his supreme calling clear" [GS 22].

The most important consequence drawn out by the Council in this regard is reflected in the declaration on religious freedom, *Dignitatis humanae,* which caused the most heated discussion in the Council. In fact, freedom of conscience and religion had been explicitly condemned by the Popes of the nineteenth century, in line with an understanding that did not recognise the relationship between freedom and truth, which, on the contrary, the Council considered to be essential. With *Dignitatis humanae* the Council put a stop to such a destructive debate, highlighting the positive aspects of the growing importance attributed to freedom in modern times and acknowledging that there is not only a right to the truth, but also the right of the person, and that the truth can only be discerned in freedom. With this understanding, the Council abandoned the doctrine of the so-called 'Catholic state' and laid the foundation for the recognition of modern pluralistic democracy.

The historical stance adopted by the Church with regard to the two above-mentioned aspects is a fundamental reference point enabling the Church and individual Christians to feel 'at home' in the modern reality. Gone is the romantic nostalgia for the Medieval period and its cohesive culture; gone is the restoration mentality following the French revolution; gone also is the regrettably zealous anti-modernism of the close of the nineteenth and start of the twentieth century.

Unfortunately, after the Council some groups fell into the opposite trap of transforming the openness of the Council into naive acquiescence. This ingenuousness had not characterised the Council itself, which had capably distinguished between legitimate autonomy and a purely secular humanism that could even be hostile to religion [GS 56]; indeed, the Council had seen atheism as one of the most alarming aspects of contemporary life (cf. GS 19-22).

Coherent consequences were drawn from this Conciliar openness by Pope Paul VI, particularly with regard to specific amendments of the Italian and Spanish concordats. With his dynamism and energy, Pope John Paul II made this vision his own, laying the foundations of a clear policy on the defence of human rights, a focus that emerged in all its strength and efficacy with respect to the totalitarian systems of the twentieth century, particularly in the ex-Soviet bloc (cf: *Redemptor hominis,*17).

Nonetheless, it soon became evident that these new tendencies needed to be defended on quite a different front. In 1965, when the Pastoral Constitution was promulgated, there was still real tension between the liberal world and totalitarian communism, although the Church had never explicitly condemned the latter, given its concern for Christians living behind the Iron Curtain. At the time, no one could have foreseen the collapse of the communist bloc and that in its aftermath the world would have to come to terms with an escalating sense of freedom and at the same time a profound loss of orientation.

In the process of secularisation, the positive fruits of modernity have been eradicated from their Christian roots; as fruits of the tree of Christianity, they now risk rotting and becoming toxic. Indeed, this has already happened. The celebrated ideals of modernity have been stripped of their transcendental roots, and have lost their secure foundation. With its emancipation from the

Church, the state has had to relinquish the resilient connective tissue that in the past had been permeated by a transcendental consciousness. At the same time; we have seen how tolerance and freedom can be displaced by a totalitarian stance towards those who defend traditional values. It would be naive not to bear in mind *The Drama of Atheistic Humanism* (H. de Lubac) and the *Dialectic of Enlightenment* (T. W. Adorno).

This should not lead us to barricade ourselves behind a new fundamentalism, which is a very real danger today. Rather, we should continue to defend the principles of the Council and to ensure that the world does not take the path of destruction. The Church should therefore present itself innovatively as an advocate for freedom in the midst of rapidly changing events. As a sign and a safeguard of the transcendence of the human person [GS 76], the Church must foster a new humanism and the authentic freedom of man. Having said this, we come to the second theme of *Gaudium et spes,* namely the vocation of the human person.

The Drama of the Threatened Dignity of the Human Person

As we have seen, the reflection of the *Pastoral Constitution on the Church in the Modern World* has as its cornerstone a focus on the human person, and clearly states: "All things on earth should be related to man as their centre and crown" [GS 12]. Thus, the Constitution assumes an unequivocally modern stance and identifies itself as being in the modern anthropological trend. Pope John Paul II himself called man "the primary and fundamental way for the Church" (*Redemptor hominis,* 14).

Naturally, the Pastoral Constitution does not take this position merely in order to adapt itself to a particular situation, but does so on the basis of fundamental theological convictions. Autonomy is not understood as separatism; man is not considered as the ultimate criterion for all things. Rather, the dignity of the human person is considered to be derived from God and founded in Jesus Christ.

Taking this as its basic premise, the Constitution develops doctrinally for the first time a coherent and structured anthropological approach. Naturally, in the past there had been some anthropological doctrinal affirmations, but there had never been a unified and systematic doctrinal line of reasoning. It should be borne in mind that from a philosophical point of view, anthropology is a relatively recent discipline, developing for the first time in the twentieth century. Therefore, in this light the Church is - so to speak - a pioneer of modern times.

It is not possible for me to comment in detail on all the anthropological affirmations of the Constitution. I will limit myself to a number of characteristic aspects, but would invite you to read from GS 11 to GS 22, as it is my opinion that these passages deserve renewed attention.

Let us take a look at the first aspect. Originally the text of the Constitution was relatively optimistic; critical perspectives were introduced only in the second phase of the debate. Thus, the definitive text speaks not only of the dignity of the human person, but also of the desolation. Due to the sin of setting himself against God, man experiences internal conflict: "As a result, all of human life, whether individual or collective, shows itself to be a dramatic struggle between good and evil, between light and darkness" [GS 13]. With this realistic and dramatic vision, the Council departs from the partial and optimistic vision of the Enlightenment, which believes in the natural goodness of man, corrupted only by the environment and social relations.

The Constitution is also realistic about the transient nature of human existence and, so to speak, looks death in the face - that death which represents the greatest human mystery (cf. GS 18). It is acutely conscious of the drama of human existence. Together with Blaise Pascal, we could say that *grandeur et misère* coexist in human nature and that the greatness of man lies in the very fact that he is aware of his misery.

There is also a second aspect: the cohesive vision of man as a union of soul and body and as a social and relational being. The Council explicitly defends the dignity of the body, and opposes itself to reductive spiritual interpretations that give rise to flawed forms of piety and ascetic practices. Yet it is critical of a materialistic anthropology. It maintains that the primacy of humans over the rest of creation lies in their spiritual nature: man transcends the material universe thanks to reason (cf. GS 14 ff.). Significantly, the Constitution affirms: "Our era needs such wisdom more than bygone ages if the discoveries made by man are to be further humanised. For the future of the world stands in peril unless wiser men are forthcoming" [GS 15].

Freedom pertains to the spiritual nature of the human being. Human dignity demands that individuals "act according to a knowing and free choice. Such a choice is personally motivated and prompted from within. It does not result from blind internal impulse nor from mere external pressure" [GS 17]. Such an affirmation is in clear contrast to an anthropology that holds that humans are animated solely by inexplicable instincts, by cerebral impulses or by biochemical mechanisms. There have been enormous changes in this context over the last sixty years: genetic engineering and modern research on embryos have raised dilemmas that were quite unimaginable in the past.

Moreover, the particular anthropological approach of the Council is one that sees man not as a monad, but as a dialogical being, in relationship with God and with others. The Constitution develops the concept that God created man in his image and likeness by affirming that in this likeness God created both male and female (cf. GS 12). Among other things, this cohesive and dialogical anthropology of the Council has led to a new personal concept of sexuality and the couple, and to a deeper understanding of marriage as a personal community and conjugal bond (cf. GS 47-52), while at the same time it has raised - together with the Encyclical *Humanae vitae* (1968) - a number of conflicts within the Church that are yet to be resolved.

The Constitution seeks to maintain and to defend the dignity of the human body and the dignity of the human being, and to reaffirm personal responsibility in the face of the trivialisation of the person and of sexuality. In this perspective, it also seeks to prevent modern subjectivism leading to self-destruction. In these terms, it is clear that the fundamental themes of the Pastoral Constitution are still of great relevance today.

The third aspect I would like to mention is the question of personal conscience, defined by the Constitution as "the most secret core and sanctuary of a man, [where he] is alone with God, whose voice echoes in his depths" [GS 16]. The conscience is the voice within the intimate being of the person, summoning one to love good and avoid evil. In these words we discern the thought of the great modern theologian John Henry Newman: "God and the soul, *cor ad cor loquitur, solus cum solo.*" This direct relationship with God enables individuals to reject any totalitarian or exclusivist claim made from outside. However, in this we also identify an internal limitation concerning an imperfectly interpreted attitude of obedience in the Church.

Yet, while the conscience is a voice that is perceptible only from within, it should not be confused with subjectivism, or with an *ad hoc* circumstantial ethic, or even less so with a blind arbitrariness. In the voice of conscience, people encounter the law "written on their hearts" (Rom. 2:14-16), the obedience to which constitutes the very dignity of man. While a subjective being, man senses an objective attribute, a moral law which ultimately identifies itself with the central message of the biblical ethic: love of God and of others.

Thus, it is easy to understand why the Council considers the personal conscience to be the fundamental reference point in dialogue with non-Christians. What unites Christians and non-Christians is not the possession of the truth, but the search for the truth. The term 'search' implies that the conscience is not an infallible reality. The Council affirms the Thomist tradition, which maintains that the conscience that errs from "invincible ignorance" does not lose its dignity. Nonetheless, it is quick to add: "The same cannot be said of a man who cares but little for truth and goodness, or of a conscience which by degrees grows practically sightless as a result of habitual sin" [GS 16]. Therefore, there can be a sinful blindness towards real values and a darkening in the heart of man.

While the affirmations on personal conscience in a certain way represent the pinnacle of the Pastoral Constitution, they are nonetheless in keeping with the traditional line of ecclesial doctrine. With these affirmations the Council touches upon the crucial issue in modern thought on subjectivism, but it neither arrives at the same point in the modern concept nor reflects consummately on the total darkness and blindness that can emerge when humanity loses the light of truth. Not only can conscience err, but it can also lose it way and be blinded, leaving humanity in darkness.

The chapter on the conscience treads a very fine line, seeking to maintain its balance without falling either one way or the other. For this very reason, the affirmations of the Council have been misinterpreted and abused on both sides. Pope John Paul II sought to develop these ideas further in his Encyclical *Veritatis splendor* (1993). Nonetheless, many points still require to be clarified and deepened; for example, the relationship between objectivism and subjectivism; between an objective norm and a concrete reality; and, above all, what natural law means in actual terms in our contemporary experience, characterised by immense cultural and social change, by confusion and by compelling external forces.

A fourth aspect concerning the Christological foundation of the anthropological approach of the Council seeks to respond to this problem. In line with Scripture, this foundation takes as its reference point the fact that the image of man in the likeness of God (cf. Gen. 1 :27) has not been destroyed but obscured by sin and has been renewed and brought to its fulfilment in Jesus Christ, who is the image of God (cf: 2 Cor. 4:4; Col. 1:15; Heb. 1:2). In fact, the Council affirms: "The truth is that only in the mystery of the incarnate Word does the mystery of man take on light" [GS 22]. The full and complete fulfilment of man's likeness to God is found in Jesus Christ. Thus, Jesus Christ is not only the revelation of the Father; he also reveals "man to man himself". The Council points out: "For by His incarnation the Son of God has united Himself in some fashion with every man" [GS 22].

In summary, the Pastoral Constitution affirms: "Such is the mystery of man, and it is a great one, as seen by believers in the light of Christian revelation. Through Christ and in Christ, the riddles of sorrow and death grow meaningful. Apart from His gospel, they overwhelm us" [GS 22]. Elsewhere we read: "But only God, who created man to His own image and ransomed him from sin, provides a fully adequate answer to these questions. This He does through what He has revealed in Christ His Son, who became man. Whoever follows after Christ, the perfect man, becomes himself more of a man" [GS 41].

This universal Christological concept was taken up and expanded upon many times by Pope John Paul II. It reflects the debate that took place in the decades before the Council on the relationship between nature and grace. Thanks to the theologians of *theologie nouvelle*, such as M. D. Chenu, H. de Lubac and others, the two-tiered classification of nature and grace developed in the seventeenth and eighteenth centuries was surpassed. These theologians returned to a prior understanding matured in late medieval thought, and particularly in Thomas Aquinas; their views were further developed within the framework of a universal Christocentric theology influenced by the new biblical and evangelical theology, and particularly by Karl Barth, perhaps the most important Protestant theologian of the twentieth century.

The current relevance of a Christocentric vision becomes evident in the light of modern pluralism, and of our own clearer understanding of this concept with respect to the past. Such a situation makes it very difficult to establish a natural moral order that is universally valid. What was once considered to be natural law is now often perceived to be merely an expression of Western culture, and, to some extent, bourgeoisie; the disintegration of Western culture in the wake of secularisation and pluralisation has meant that the concept of natural moral law can no longer be taken for granted even in the West. The Church is thus confronted by a serious dilemma: how does it transmit its message in a comprehensible and acceptable way?

As a consequence, the Council relegated the concept of natural moral law to the background, without however abandoning it (cf. GS 64, 74); indeed, the Council sought a new approach in order to safeguard it. For if universal human values no longer exist, it is impossible to establish inter religious dialogue and a peaceful understanding between the various ages and cultures. The "clash of civilisations" (S. P. Huntington) is thus inevitable. Even if we consider the issue merely in terms of peaceful coexistence, we cannot escape dealing with the question of moral law and we cannot evade a response to the question raised by the Bible and reiterated in *Gaudium et spes*: What is man? We simply cannot disregard the question raised by metaphysics in the past.

The Council was able to offer a response only by allusion. It takes a new direction by affirming that the Gospel emanates a light and an energy "which can serve to structure and consolidate the human community according to the divine law" (GS 42 ff.). This means that only in the light and energy of Christ, the new man, can we rediscover, heal and renew the authentic humanity of mankind and construct a new humanism. It is in this sense that we are able to understand the meaning of dialogical thought and prophetic language. The Council was able only to allude to this new methodology and new synthesis; it therefore represents only the start of the journey and not the end. *Gaudium et spes* challenges us to go ahead.

Gaudium et spes as a Starting Point and Future Perspectives

Despite its limitations, the Pastoral Constitution offered a new and important direction for the Church in its journey towards the twenty-first century and the third millennium. It is true that the magisterium had already addressed specific issues and social questions such as marriage and the family, war and peace. However, the Second Vatican Council abandoned the defensive restoration mentality it had assumed after the French Revolution. The Council strove to overcome obsolete aspirations originating from particular historical conditions and sought to lay the basis for a new inculturation of Christianity in the modern world. This new constructive and dialogical approach was not uncritical and naive; rather, we can speak of a prophetic vision radiated by the light of the Gospel of Jesus Christ.

In this perspective, the Constitution was in tune with a free, democratic post-Enlightenment world, realistically recognising the legitimate autonomy of culture, human rights, and the freedom of conscience and religion. However, this was not simply in order to conform with the new reality. It was not compelled to take these steps, merely accepting and approving developments that had already taken place; it did so independently, in line with its own principles and maintaining a critical attitude. The Constitution did, however, illustrate that Christians had no reason either to confront modern developments *only* in a negative way or to remain bound to blinkered generalisations. We do well to take up the invitation of the Apostle Paul: "Test everything; hold fast to what is good" (1 Thess. 5:21).

This new direction in content reflects a new direction in methodology and a new type of magisterial document. The 'pontifical style' of previous encyclicals is abandoned in favour of a less abstract and deductive approach; there emerges a more empirical and concrete form, a dialogical style based on a more prophetic language. In his numerous encyclicals, Pope John Paul made this style his own, conferring his own particular mark. In this light as well, it is clear that it is no longer possible to go backwards, to return to the past.

Naturally, the Pastoral Constitution could not foresee the passage from the modern period to our contemporary post-modern reality, with its new challenges and new problems. This development has not only brought into question the Christian heritage but also the very ideals of modernism itself. The contemporary post-modern period has lost sight of the profound relationship between freedom and truth. Particularly in the West, we have witnessed an erosion of traditional values and a widespread loss of orientation. The Council certainly could not have foreseen the consequences of the post-colonial period in the Third World. The concept of the independence of the Church from any given cultural or political system [GS 42] may be considered to have had a strong impact in these countries and to have contributed to the rejection of a traditional Eurocentrism. Therefore, the Pastoral Constitution helped to give a new, let us say, catholic shape to the universal Church; indeed, thanks to it, for the first time the Church in reality became a world Church.

After the enormous changes of the last sixty years, we should ask ourselves what the Pastoral Constitution means today. We most certainly cannot put ourselves into reverse gear and return to the purely defensive attitude of the past. Nor can we remain at a standstill. The methodology and fundamental principles of the Constitution are still valid today, but they must be seen in the light of our contemporary context and must be applied anew in a prophetic way. It is not merely a question of making space for the legitimate concerns of our era; rather, it is a question of defending and safeguarding our values from self-destruction. In this sense, the Church today is not the opponent but the ally of freedom, the twin sister of truth. In this same sense, we are today - the Council reminds us - not only the witnesses to the birth of a new humanism [GS 55] but also the advocates of a new humanism and a new culture of life, of solidarity and of love.

We are dealing with questions that go well beyond the Pastoral Constitution, and their clarification requires further, more extensive reflection - one that *Gaudium et spes* cannot possibly offer. Important reflections can be found in the Encyclical *Fides et ratio* (1998), which takes up some of the salient ideas that have marked the passage from modern idealism to the post-idealism of the later philosophy of Schelling and - together with Mohler and Newman - of the brilliant Antonio Rosmini, one of the great prophetic spirits of the nineteenth century, who has fortunately been rehabilitated and who deserves to be rediscovered as a valuable resource for our modern crisis. However, lingering on this point would be straying too far from our path.

While future developments are impossible to envisage today, they must not take the form of a ghost journey into the universe, where the Church is like a rocket projected into infinite space with no-one left on earth to guarantee its control. We must learn to re-read *Gaudium et spes* in a new way, concerning ourselves with the principles it has outlined or at least called to mind; these principles must be further developed with patience and determination through painstaking theological work aiming at their courageous implementation in the contemporary context, in both a constructive and critical way.

Together with *Dignitatis humanae* and other documents, *Gaudium et spes* ushered in a new era in the history of the Church in a rapidly changing world. The Pastoral Constitution prepared the way for the Gospel in the twenty-first century, recalling and epitomising the words of one of my favourite Church Fathers, Irenaeus of Lyons: "The glory of God is the living being" (*Adversus Haereses* IV, 20, 7).

GOD IN THE WORLD: THE DYNAMIC PRESENCE OF CHRIST AND THE SPIRIT IN *GAUDIUM ET SPES*

Dr. James Hanvey SJ argues that a key achievement of *Gaudium et spes* is a recovery of the world and a revaluation of the secular. Its vision of the dynamic immanent economy of grace opens up a previously abstract metaphysics to more existential and relational concepts focused on the person of Christ and the activity of the Holy Spirit, making available a more scripturally determined understanding of salvation history as the unfolding of the Divine salvific presence in human history. This reaches its climax in the sanctification of the human person: the *imago Dei*, called into communion not only with God but also with neighbour. The universal common good is ultimately the redeemed *communio* of the human race and the world is thus the realm in which we are called to the work of human redemption. In this context, atheism is a question of the nature and ontological security of the human person, and the drama of human existence is also the drama of the Spirit within history, bringing about the kingdom of Christ.

"It would be ungracious if we were not to praise the efforts of the Commission which has produced the document we are now considering. There can be no doubt that the Council Fathers concerned and their advisers have worked hard and have done their best. It is nevertheless quite obvious that the document they have presented to us is unworthy of a General Council of the Church ... What sort of judgement, venerable Brothers, do you think the world will pass on this treatise? On some questions, as we know, it is better to say too little than too much. On the subject of world problems, however, it would have been much better to say nothing than produce a set of platitudes ... I must speak plainly. This document is going to dash the hopes of eveyone who has been awaiting it."[1]

This was the judgement of John, Cardinal Heenan on the first draft of the *Pastoral Constitution on the Church in the Modern World*. Today we are familiar with its vision and themes; they have helped shape the Church's self-understanding for the last forty years. Yet, *Gaudium et spes* was not a planned document. It arose out of the experience of the Council itself and it required both a new way of speaking and a new methodology.[2]

It also has to be read in conjunction with the *Dogmatic Constitution on the Church, Lumen gentium*. If *Lumen gentium* is concerned with the essence and mystery of the Church, *Gaudium et spes* is concerned with the life of the Church in all the structures of human society and culture. This is a more subtle and complex relationship than simply speaking about its mission, though it certainly includes it. Rather, it is the insight that the Church is integral to the whole salvific economy. As God's redeeming activity permeates every aspect of human existence and history so, in some sense, the Church too is present and active. This relationship does not absorb the Church into culture but neither does it set it over against it. *Lumen gentium* uses the scriptural images of seed and leaven, and that dynamic vision is amplified in *Gaudium et spes*: at local, national and international levels the Church is positively active in helping to build human cultures and societies. Yet, it is not an agent of some ideological movement, it is the

---

[1]   Bulletino, Heythrop Archives, Vatican II.

[2]   Its final form was the result of close collaboration between the theological experts and lay experts.

witness to God's purpose in history; it is itself the first fruits of that redeemed society, the Kingdom, to which every human being is invited. How does one express this without either simply falling back upon a destructive dualism (Church versus 'the world') or compromising the fact that the Church is God's work, not a human product?

A New Methodology

The structure of *Gaudium et spes* reflects an attempt to address this problem. The Constitution is divided into two parts. The first sets out the theological basis of the Church's presence in the world, seeking to interpret the meaning of the human person and the existential condition of humanity in the light of Christ. This establishes that the Church's position is not that of a neutral or disengaged observer: the Church speaks from her understanding of Christ but from within the movement of culture and history.

Part I [GS 1-45] describes the Church's solidarity with humanity and its mission to bring it to its ultimate fulfilment in Christ. On the one hand, there is a fractured, anxious human existence *"usque ad mortem"*, marked by the reality of sin, the temptation to atheism and nihilism. On the other, is the joy that comes from knowing Christ and accepting his gift of the Spirit of life. Part II [GS 46-93] selects central themes and concerns for society and the international order and thinks them through in the light of the insights and principles established in Part I.

In keeping with the general methodology of the Council, there is no attempt to identify *adversarii* (enemies or opponents) and pronounce anathemas. There is, however, a searching critique in which the Church enters into a dialogue with the secular world, especially its understanding of the human person, the purpose of human life and the nature of human society.[3] In this, *Gaudium et spes* does not offer a fixed form, but one that is flexible and dynamic, willing to learn; to appropriate as well as to reject and condemn. It is a method which attempts to recognise the existential and historical situation in which the writing takes place.

Underlying this methodology, is an understanding of Revelation as a dynamic process which, though always available in Christ and therefore essentially stable, is nevertheless grasped in every situation in a fluid and contingent way.[4] This interplay between Revelation and historical existence discloses the active economy of Revelation that shapes history and cultures. It was an insight of *Lumen gentium* that the Church itself is part of this economy and that is why the Church is always part of history, not just sociologically but as the 'seed of the Kingdom'. *Gaudium et spes* rejects an escape to an a-historical realm of pure essences in favour of a confident, open engagement with the world and history. It acknowledges the fluidity of the human search for understanding which can be realised in structures that promote and sustain the universal common good.

This shift in method represents a shift in the way we think of the Church as located in history. The usual binary or oppositional dialectic - sacred/secular, time/eternity, Church/world, body/soul - is reconfigured in a way that attempts to grasp a more complex relationship of dynamic mutuality. In a sense, it is an effort to apply

---

[3] Although this is an innovative approach for Conciliar documents it represents a return to an older dialogical form of apologetics. This is best exemplified by Augustine in his engagement with the Roman culture of the late Empire of which the classic example is his book, *The City of God.*

[4] The possibility of this approach was prepared in the *Dogmatic Constitution on Divine Revelation, Dei Verbum.* Cf. R. Murray, Revelation (*Dei Verbum*), in A. Hastings (ed.) (London, Modern Catholicism, SPCK 1990), pp. 74-83.

the Christological paradigm - the unity in distinction of the two natures in the Person of Christ - to our way of understanding historical and cultural existence. Here we can see the radical and thoroughgoing application of Christology in *Gaudium et spes*. The memorable and critical formula of Chalcedon, "one and the same Christ, Son, Lord, only-begotten acknowledged in two natures which undergo no confusion, no change, no division, no separation ... " is now explicitly the epistemological principle by which we not only understand the action of grace but discover the hermeneutical principle for reading "the signs of the times".[5]

This very paradigm requires an attentiveness to the graced dynamics of historical movements and social circumstances.[6] This "new" approach lies behind the Council's decision to introduce the genre of a "pastoral" Constitution.[7] In other words, a genuine historical awareness cannot simply reach for binding definitions but must seek broad hermeneutical orientations which are

---

[5] From Tanner, N.P., (ed.), *Decrees of the Ecumenical Councils Vol. 1* (London, Sheed & Ward Limited, 1990), p 86. The Council of Chalcedon (451 AD) sets the terms for Christology in its understanding of the relations of the divine and human natures constituting the one person of Christ. Cf. also the *Tome of Leo* where the principle is expressed: "There is nothing unreal about this oneness, since both the lowliness of the man and the grandeur of the divinity are in mutual relation. As God is not changed by showing mercy, neither is the humanity devoured by the dignity it received. The activity of each form (*forma*) is what is proper to it in communion with the other ..." (Tanner: 79.) What is described here is the perichoresis of natures. All subsequent quotations are taken from Tanner.

[6] GS: 5; 74.

[7] For detailed discussion and commentary on this aspect of the *Constitution,* cf. Charles Moeller's 'History of the Constitution' in *Commentary on the Documents of Vatican II Vol. 5*, ed. Vorgrimler, H. (London, Burns and Oates, 1969), pp. 1-76 (hereafter Vorgrimler); also, Rahner, K. 'On The Theological Problems entailed in a "Pastoral Constitution"', Theo. Invest. Vol. X, E.T. David Bourke, New York, Seabury Press, 1977, pp. 293-317.

capable of providing guidance. There cannot be specific and precise answers in advance. We can have principles, but, in the best sense, we have also to improvise, seeking to be guided by the activity of Divine Wisdom. For this reason the Constitution does not see itself as a completed work, rather it is one which continues to be written in the praxis and reflection which it initiates. This open-endedness can appear to be a weakness, and it can also make *Gaudium et spes* appear to be the fruit of a naïve optimism about the world and the forces that are shaping it. I believe such a view is mistaken. To be sure the Constitution has its weaknesses, but we should not think of it as lacking in methodological and theological sophistication.[8]

Revaluation of the World

If *Gaudium et spes* is innovative in its methodology, it is radical in its revaluation of the world. This is an aspect of the Constitution which is little commented on. To appreciate it we have to remind ourselves of the long history of *contemptus mundi* which conditions Christian

---

[8]   See Rowland, Tracey, *Culture and the Thomist Tradition: After Vatican II* (London , Routledge, 2003). Rowland argues that the Council, and *Gaudium et spes* in particular, lacked a theology of culture and therefore gave grounds for a naïve accommodation with modernism. Divorcing the Church from a tradition with its own criteria of truth and rationality, it thus severed faith from reason, nature from grace and sacred from secular. Subsequent calls for a 'relevant' approach to pastoral issues therefore offered a concept that was empty of content (cf. pp 2, 18, 72 ff.). Rowland marshals a very full and disparate array of criticisms against *Gaudium et spes* but, at its deepest level, her concern is with the relationship between grace and culture. She argues for an 'Augustinian Thomist' conception, based on 'a "root and branch" kind of renewal encapsulated by Pickstock's juxtaposition of the "polity of death" with a "liturgical city".' (cf. pp. 21, 167 – 168). In contrast, my argument here is that the Council's theological framework, clearly expressed in the concept of '*imago Dei*' and its dynamic understanding of the economy which underpins *Gaudium et spes*, is designed precisely to overcome such a dualism.

thought and life prior to the Council. Typically, this sees "the World" as a dangerous and hostile place for Christians. Indeed, in the New Testament, although the Johannine and Pauline writings characterize 'the world' in different ways, they converge in their understanding of it as an alien kingdom, an "anti-kingdom" which Christians are exhorted to reject and flee. This is in line with the dramatic character of Christian existence in its sense of being in a battle with destructive forces opposed to Christ. At root, these forces are spiritual but they manifest themselves in history, being encountered by Christians both in their personal spiritual struggle to express the triumph of Christ in their lives and also in the material and historical struggle, in the face of persecutions and repressions, against those who would destroy all forms of Christian existence.[9] In this context the "spiritual" life takes on a triumphant eschatological value over against the "worldly" life. If, in its original understanding, this drama was lived *in the world* we can see how it comes to underpin and justify a flight *from the world*. This is given concrete expression in the ascetical forms of religious monastic and eremitical life. Indeed, it is the purpose of ascetical practices to overcome the concupiscence which attaches us to the world, distracting us from pure service of God - the becoming the "spiritual man or woman" - that the kingdom requires.[10]

Given this understanding, we can see how the interior life comes to be prioritised and valued over the exterior one. This then determines the relationship of the sacred to the secular.[11] The hierarchical system of values

---

[9]   Note on the "Powers and Principalities" : cf. especially Heinrich Schlier's essay written after the experience of Hitler. Heinrich Schlier, *Principalities and Powers in the New Testament*, Fribourg, *Quaestiones Disputatae* 3. Herder, Nelson 1961.
[10]   Cf. Thomas Aquinas, *ST.* I-II q.77 a.5; q. 108, a.3 ad 4; q.108. a 4 c.
[11]   McGinn, B., (ed.), *Christian Spirituality Origins To The Twelfth Century* (London, Routledge & Kegan Paul, 1986), 153-155.

flowing from the former to the latter further underpins states of life within the Church. This is most clearly seen in Gratian's code, which only recognises the Bishop and religious. The laity has only a negative definition, being defined as those who are not in Holy Orders or Religious Life.[12] Thus there is a strong evaluative dualism - sacred/secular, eternal/temporal, contemplative/active - in which mundane life and activity has no significant value in its own right. Of course, this not only maps a hierarchy of value but of power.

The problem, then, of how to value "secular" activity becomes acute. There may be mechanisms for "redeeming the secular" in terms of the transference of goods - the exchange of material goods for "spiritual capital" through alms and benefactions etc., - but moral value still lies with the spiritual. We can see this at its clearest in the division of powers in the medieval world where Kings ruled over "bodies" but priests had jurisdiction over "souls". Of course, I Cor. 3.15 - the spiritual man judges all things and is himself judged by no one - was invoked to assure spiritual supremacy.[13] We can see here, already, the creation of the "secular" world. Indeed, it is possible to argue that the Church itself is, to an extent, the creator of the secular. In this order of things the secular has no autonomy and can only find its value in relation to the sacred. It is this which also informs the priority given to the contemplative life over the active one.[14]

---

[12] Although the laity receives a positive theology in Vatican II and the mission which they have, grounded in the sacrament of baptism, continues to be deepened in the reflections of the Magisterium (cf. *Christifideles Laici*, John Paul II, 1988), the negative definition still continues to be present.

[13] Cf Congar, "The Role Of The Church In The Modern World" in Vorgrimler, pp. 202-223, esp. pp. 203-207.

[14] Again it is Thomas Aquinas who both articulates the tradition and extols it in the priority he gives to the contemplative life. The key text is the Gospel account of Martha and Mary (Lk.10. 38-42) and

If, broadly speaking, we can accept this account, we can see in it the origins of a secular modernity. The "modern world" is constituted precisely in breaking free of the sacred as the source of its value and asserting its own independence. The mechanism for this self-valuation is "autonomy" or "freedom" and this becomes the primary touchstone value of the modern world. This is a momentous cultural, intellectual and existential revolution. Having claimed its independence and established not only its intellectual autonomy but also its own self-valuation, the secular world radically separates itself from the 'sacred.' It no longer has any need of it in order to legitimate its value and, indeed, the secular can see in the claims of the sacred a threat to its own freedom and worth. The counter process now ensues, whereby it is the "sacred", especially as represented by the institution of the Church and the metaphysics which support its hierarchy of values, which is devalued. The secular will revalue the ordinary in its own terms; it no longer requires the "spiritual". This begins the process of secularisation. Here, it will be useful to distinguish the "secular" from the process of secularisation in order to appreciate the task facing *Gaudium et spes* and the nature of its achievement.

The process of secularisation goes beyond distinguishing the secular from the sacred; it claims the self-sufficient autonomy of the secular. In other words, in addition to being a Weberian description of the separation of the sacred/secular spheres in the social realm, it becomes an ideological process which is concerned to

---

Thomas' commentary on it as justifying the superiority of the contemplative life. III Sent d 35 q 1. ST II-II q.179-182, 188. The contemplative life is ordered directly and immediately to the love of God and hence care about exterior actions and their execution hinders the contemplative life, (II-II q 182 a 2 3c). Cf. Also Von Balthasar, H. U., 'Action and Contemplation' in *Explorations In Theology I: The Word Made Flesh* (San Fransico, Ignatius Press, 1989), pp. 227-240.

erase religion, understanding it to be hostile to the autonomy of the secular. It is not uncommon for religion, whether institutional or personal, to be portrayed as the enemy of knowledge, freedom and human progress. Given an aggressive doctrine of secularisation the Church is faced with a profound dilemma: it either allows itself to be characterised as the enemy of the secular, or it must find a new way of valuing it, without selling out to secularisation. The temptation to the former is considerable, for it is easy to understand in terms of the old struggle against the world. In this version the Church is rejected and in exile; it must accept its loss of power, becoming again "the little flock" that flees to the desert. If it does not do this, it must find a new value for the secular and reconceptualise its relation to the "sacred" in terms which do not allow a new devaluation of the world. A way must be found to recognise that the secular is not necessarily antipathetic to the sacred nor, indeed, is it immune to holiness. Here is the significance of the Incarnation and recovering the dynamic integration of grace and nature. We only come to the secular in a resistant or obstructive way if we are working from premises that are not informed by Revelation.[15]

In addition to this realignment *ad extra* the Church must reconstruct its valuation of the "ordinary" *ad intra*. Internally, this will entail a reconstruction of the hierarchical ordering of values. The spirituality of the community and the metaphysics which support it, all constructed around "contempt for the world" will also

---

[15] According to Karl Rahner the non-oppositional character of nature and grace has its highest expression in the Incarnation which is simultaneously the revelatory source of our knowledge of this non-opposition. Cf. Rahner, K., *Theological Investigations Vol 1: God, Christ, Mary And Grace* (London, Darton Longman and Todd, 1961), pp 164 n.1,165.

have to change.[16]   I believe that the tensions in our theologies of the relationship between priesthood and laity, the vocation to religious life and the vocation to the "ordinary" life of marriage, children, and work, can be traced to this re-orientation to the "secular".

Even in such brief outline one can appreciate the enormous pressures that the Church faces intellectually as well as culturally. This is the context in which we need to understand the achievement and the stress lines that run through *Gaudium et spes*. The extent to which it represents a recovery of the world and a revaluation of the secular is often not appreciated. That revaluation is essential for the full realisation of the theology of the laity developed in *Lumen gentium* and articulated in the universal call to holiness which stands at its centre.[17]   In both these interdependent and central themes, *Gaudium et spes* works with a vision of the dynamic immanent economy of grace which allows for theology of *personal* divine presence.   This opens up previously largely abstract metaphysics of nature and grace and Trinity to more directly personal existential and relational concepts focused on the person of Christ and the activity of the Holy Spirit. A more scripturally determined understanding of salvation history as the unfolding of the dynamic of the Divine salvific presence in human history is now available. It reaches its climax in the sanctification of the human person.[18]

---

[16]   Though in a less obvious way, *Perfectae caritatis,* the Council's decree on renewal of Religious life, is the other text in which this revaluation may be observed.

[17]   Cf. *Lumen gentium*, chapter 5.

[18]   Some have seen in this the influence of Teilhard de Chardin with his understanding of Christ as the formal and final cause (the Alpha and Omega) in the evolutionary process of humanity, and grace as the immanent power or energy which brings it about. In some sense, of course, Teilhard provides an important conceptual framework for understanding the immanent dynamism of the Divine economy that is active in created matter and human freedom. Yet,

Christological Anthropology: the *Imago Dei*

The human person as the *imago Dei* stands at the centre of *Gaudium et spes*.[19] It is a theological anthropology

---

Gaudium et spes is also cautious about giving wholesale approval to the Teilhardian thesis. If anything, it draws much more from the thought of Chenu and Congar, particularly Congar's thesis of the increasing personalisation of revelation in The Mystery of the Temple. Here, Congar argues that salvation history is the progressive transference of the Divine presence from the exterior to the interior reaching its climax in Christ through whom the Holy Spirit is "poured into our hearts" so that the new place of the Divine is the in-dwelling of the Holy Spirit in the human person. This line of thought is further reinforced by an understanding of grace as constitutive of human nature along the lines developed by Henri de Lubac and Karl Rahner, to name its most prominent advocates. Cf. Ratzinger, J., "The Dignity Of The Human Person" in Vorgrimler, pp. 115-163 and my article 'In the Presence of Love: The Pneumatological Realization of the Economy: Yves Congar's *Le Mystère du Temple*' in *International Journal of Systematic Theology,* 2005, October, Vol. 7, No. 4, pp. 383-398. Also, for Chenu and the whole approach of La Saulchoir cf. *Une école de théologie. Le Saulchoir* (Paris, Du Cerf, 1937 reprinted with commentaries by Alberigo, A G. et. al. Paris, Du Cerf, 1985). It is important to note that Teilhard's thought was very much within the context of French *nouvelle théologie* of the time. For a useful critical discussion of the theological structure of Teilhard's thought, cf. Von Balthasar, H. U., *Theo-drama,Vol. V: The Last Act (*San Francisco, Ignatius Press, 1998), pp 153 -168. Chenu, drawing upon A. Gardiel's seminal *Le Donné Révéle et La Théologie* (1909, reissued in 1932 with an introduction by Chenu) will argue that *"L'humanisation est la voie de la divinisation"* cited in Potworowski, C. *Contemplation and Incarnation, The Theology of Marie-Dominique Chenu* (Montreal, McGill University Press, 2001), p.83. The whole chapter, 'Christianity and History', in Potworowski's study is not only informative on Chenu but useful for the context of French theological ideas which come to the fore in the Council.

[19] A useful and comprehensive theological treatment of the whole "*imago Dei*" tradition is to be found in, Argimiro Turrado, *Dios en el Hombre, Plenitud o tragedia* (Madrid, BAC 1971). Turrado makes the point that the '*imago dei*'is critical for our understanding of the inhabitation of the Divine life in the redeemed (grace) which is a restoration of the image in the justified. Particularly useful is his treatment of the development of the notion of the *imago Dei* in Augustine and its subsequent use in Luther, pp. 261 ff. However,

which has shaped the tradition but, set within the context of a dynamic immanence of the Divine Presence effectively an implicit pneumatology the *imago Dei* itself must be understood afresh, in a dynamic way. If the *imago* is constitutive of the human person then it is the movement within each individual for fulfilment and actualisation. The human person is never instrumentalised in the Divine economy but called into an active partnership (son/daughtership) which restores a disordered freedom so that the person can be fully responsive to Divine grace.

Gaudium et spes also understands this exercise of our freedom to have a social and interpersonal dimension, so that the *imago Dei* is not reduced to a single detached subject but grasped ultimately in the social sphere. This reality, which is ontologically grounded as our ultimate destiny, is what makes all human beings, irrespective of their status, race, capacity, or economic power of equal and irreducible value. The *imago Dei* is not simply a passive property but a moral imperative: it makes everyone my neighbour and worthy of my respect and charity. There is a deep unity between our *vocatio* - to be called into communion with God - and our *communio* with one another. This dynamic is nothing less than love and our participation in the God who is Love, so that love is the ground and form of what it is to be human, as it is also the essence of God's own Triune life. In this respect, the mystery of the Church is rooted in the Divine *communio* of the Trinity. The *telos* of humanity is social, for the fulfilment of *fraternitas* is the *communio sanctorum*.[20] It is

---

although Turrado explores the ecclesial aspects of this 'in-dwelling' he does not expand upon its social and communitarian aspects which is a major contribution and development to the idea in *Gaudium et spes*, as I have attempted to indicate here. The Constitution begins to sketch the social nature of justification.

[20] GS 18; 24-25; 32. This is an important development which further integrates *Gaudium et spes* with the insights of *Lumen gentium* and corrects the previous tendencies to see sanctification in

for this reason that *Gaudium et spes* understands the Church's presence and mission in the world as the building up of a human *communio* expressed historically and socially in all the structures of international solidarity: the universal common good is ultimately the redeemed *communio* of the human race.

In this way, the ecclesiology of *Gaudium et spes* is a further development of the ecclesiology of *Lumen gentium*. For *Lumen gentium* the Church is the universal sacrament of salvation, and this is a significant context for understanding the way in which *Gaudium et spes* develops and locates the "common good."[21] To do full justice to this theme is beyond the scope of the present essay but it would be important to notice that the "common good" also has a soteriological dimension which has not been fully acknowledged in treatments of it.[22]

---

personal terms. Here, the idea of a human solidarity is translated not only into the ethics of social realm but ultimately ordered to the eschatological vision of the *communio sanctorum*: the redeemed society of humanity. Cf. Semmelroth, O., 'The Community Of Mankind' in Vorgrimler, pp.164-181.

[21]   GS 45; Also citing LG, Chapter 2.

[22]   For the first time in Catholic Social Teaching, *Gaudium et spes* offers a definition of the Common Good (cf. § 26; 74). These are also elements not sufficiently recognised by Tracey Rowland in her criticism of *Gaudium et spes*. It is for this reason that she fails to appreciate the implicit unity that runs through the Constitution of the 'common good' and the *communio*/solidarity. In this sense, *Gaudium et spes* is much more radical and innovative than is recognised because it has an undeveloped but significant grasp of the common good as not just a 'natural' principle but a soteriological dynamic. Two useful discussions of the 'common good' are, Porter, J., 'The Common Good in Thomas Aquinas', pp. 94-120. and McCann, D. P., 'The Common Good in Catholic Social Teaching', pp. 121-146 to be found in *In Search of the Common Good,* (ed.) by. Miller, P. and McCann, D. P. (New York/London, T & T Clark International, 2005). Although Porter argues that Aquinas understands the common good in terms of the exercise of political authority, she does accept that it is integral to the exercise of charity. But this needs to be developed because for Aquinas charity does not only have a practical social or

These moves lay the foundation for the recovery of the social and secular realms and the revaluation of secular activity.

In understanding the social dimension of the *imago*, *Gaudium et spes* can value human political and cultural activity. It can also understand that the exercise of freedom not only has an ethical intention in pursuit of the personal and common good but is grounded in a theological insight into the unity of the good and the holy. Therefore, the secular realm is recovered as the theatre of our sanctification, individually and collectively. Thus, *Gaudium et spes* does not abandon the world but reclaims it. As I have understood its strategy, it does not degrade the legitimate autonomy of the secular but recovers its purpose and value. This is achieved by an understanding of the interplay between grace and freedom. This is rooted in the Constitution's incarnational vision, which always reads humanity and human history in the context of Christ and the active economy of the Holy Spirit. In other words, *Gaudium et spes* responds to Modernity positively, by refusing the dualism of sacred and secular and positing a graced interplay of these fields. It offers a high vision of the human person and society through a Christological humanism. It significantly recovers the notion of freedom from a secular Modernity and reinterprets it pneumatologically in terms of humanity's ordination to holiness, that is, to God. The "good society" can only be so if it strives to be the "holy society", for only this will provide the structures and orientations for genuine human flourishing: the cherishing of the *imago Dei* in each person and the seeking of God who is the ultimate and lasting Good. In these various

---

political goal but one that is teleological and soteriological. Our ultimate purpose is the participation in the Trinitarian life of Charity that is the complete good. Society is realised in the friendship with God and with each other which is a '*communicatio in bono*' (ST.II-II 25.3).

ways *Gaudium et spes* realigns the Church in terms of Modernity and the meaning of secularisation. It also recovers for the Church the intrinsic unity between love of God and love of neighbour as an incarnational dynamic - an *imitatio Christi* - rather than a purely ethical commandment.

In this way, political, scientific, artistic and civil life can be shaped in terms of the Divine economy of salvation. Indeed, this must be so if the "*imago Dei*" as a social and interpersonal reality is to be realised. Yet, this does not mean that the Church has some *a priori* blueprint; rather, there is always the creative, indeed redemptive, action of graced human freedom. Grace makes the human person a genuine "maker" and hence the old hierarchy of the *vita contemplative* having priority over the *vita activa* can no longer apply.[23] The "world" is not a place to flee from but the realm in which we are called to the new work of human redemption and sanctification. This will be played out in the works of justice, peace, the recognition of the sacred value of human life, the dignity of the human person, the defence of universal human rights, the struggle to overcome

---

[23]   This revaluation is an important corrective, which means that the Church is no longer subject to the criticisms made by a writer like Hannah Arendt in *The Human Condition* (New York, Doubleday Anchor, 1959) of valuing the contemplative life over the active life. Arendt's determination to value and defend the active life lies in her perception that it is necessary to restore and value the integrity of the political sphere - freedom. The purpose of politics is freedom and its field of experience is action. Without this society will always live in danger of totalitarianisms. In *Gaudium et spes,* the active life is valued but it is not seen in opposition to the contemplative life. Rather, as the contemplative life is a mirror of the Divine Life it is not static or inactive but precisely the actualisation of Love which is creative as the plenitude of Goodness. Thus the contemplative life follows from participation in the Good into action the purpose and end of which is the generation of love or Charity. For *Gaudium et spes* all Christian action in the world that flows is the expression of the sanctifying dynamic of the Holy Spirit.

poverty and oppression, the ordering of technology to the lasting universal human good, and the upholding of the rights of the family.

Drama as a Critical Category[24]

In this context the question of atheism becomes acute. Given the vision set out in *Gaudium et spes,* it is not sufficient to read it purely in terms of unbelief in God. Nor should it be seen as the triumph of rationalism which liberates humanity from mytho-poetic illusions and the oppressive, counter-progressive demands of organised religion. It cannot portray itself as the expression of secular autonomy because the Incarnation refuses to allow us to read the destiny of God independently from the destiny of humanity. Atheism, therefore, becomes a question about what it is to be human and about the ultimate value of human action.[25] It is essentially the drama between humanity and God in which the very nature and ontological security of the human person is at stake. In a most vivid way, atheism brings to the surface the soteriological drama of history made explicit through the ideological credos and movements of the eighteenth, nineteenth and twentieth centuries.[26] From its place in

---

[24]   GS 10 ff.

[25]   The way in which *Gaudium et spes* treats atheism is, of course, already anticipated in Paul VI's *Ecclesiam suam.* These themes had already been developed in the writings of theologians before the Council but perhaps the most influential was de Lubac's , *Le drame de l'humanisme athée* (Paris, Spes, 1945), (ET Sheed and Ward, London, 1950). *Gaudium et spes* incorporates de Lubac's thesis that atheism is contrary to humanity. Cf. also Ratzinger, 'The Dignity Of The Human Person' in Vorgrimler, pp.146-155.

[26]   Nietzsche is of particular representative significance here. Of the many texts that may be cited § 215 -217, "War against the Christian ideal, against the doctrine of blessedness and salvation as the goal of life, against the supremacy of the simple, the pure in heart, the suffering and unfortunate..." in *The Will To Power*, ed. and trans. Walter Kaufmann (New York, Random House, 1967). The Nietschean atheism or anti-Christian polemic is a major influence on de Lubac

history, the Council is acutely aware that these ideologies have not only been theological and philosophical but have taken cultural and political forms in Nazism and Communism. For the Church, the logic is consistent: ultimately if atheism seeks to erase God, it will seek to erase his image in humanity. So there is a fundamental flaw in the idea of a humanistic atheism. It can only make sense if atheism is also engaged in rearticulating what it is to be human. If this is granted, then this 'atheistic construct', precisely because it is a construct, will always leave the human unstable and vulnerable to further 'constructions' depending on the dominant ideology and its needs. On the surface, atheism may be seductively offered as liberation, but it will soon reveal itself as an enslavement in which humanity is instrumentalised.

Humanity can only have an ontological security which grounds personal, social, economic, cultural and religious existence when it accepts its theological character: it carries the Divine image - the image of Christ.[27] This is the reason why Christology and anthropology cannot be thought apart.[28]

---

and his counter formulation of Christian humanism. Cf. the extensive engagement with Nietzsche in *Le drame de l'humanisme athée*,

[27] This also forms the basis of human rights. Cf.GS18 also 24, 25, 32. There is here, too, another grounding of universal Human Rights. Cf. *Pacem in terris*, esp. § 60, John XXIII. These themes are taken up again in GS and will be enlarged in the writings of John Paul II, especially '*fraternitas*' as solidarity and '*communio.*' Important in this respect is the way in which John Paul II analyses structural sin in regard to the universal common good. (Cf. e.g. *Sollicitudo rei socialis*, 1987 § 36.) CF. Erhueh, A.O., *Vatican II Image of God in Man* (Rome, Urbaniana University Press, 1986) who describes these themes. However he does not probe them or the significant development that GS represents.

[28] This unity is essentially the basis of the doctrine of grace and the dynamic soteriology which informs the whole Constitution. Christ is the perfect image of the Father and so the '*imago Dei*' in us is the image of Christ. The more we are conformed to Christ the more

An important and related dimension of the theological anthropology sketched in *Gaudium et spes* is the concept of *interioritas* or "inwardness".[29] This was an innovative word, although it has a long history in Catholic thought. Some commentators have understood it in terms of "conscience".[30] But this is a limited reading which misses its significance. Although it clearly does embrace conscience, it is also has a much wider implication. It draws upon the Augustinian tradition whereby inwardness is essential to our ability to discern truth, especially in relation to God. It is a capacity of the soul and, contra the Cartesian turn inward to the "ego", the solitary "I", it is a turn inward, a point of freedom from the flux of time, to the point of convergence of relationships with God and the realities of the world. The God that is encountered in this inner space is not a private property but the God that is a good common to all souls. For Augustine, inwardness or *interioritas* has a social dimension: it is a turning to the community of souls who glimpse the same truth; there is an inner unity of all good souls bound together by love of God, which was the original state of all before the fall.[31] As we have seen, this dimension is also present in *Gaudium et spes* but the Constitution uses it also as a way to distinguish the human person in his or her particularity that prevents a reductive materialism. Thus, recognising the "interiority" which characterises the human person is not only a way of grounding uniqueness, as a species as well as individually, it is also a way of resisting atheism, which evacuates this inwardness by denying its foundation in the person's orientation to God

---

human we become because we realise more completely the image that we are.

[29]   Cf. Ratzinger, 'The Dignity Of The Human Person' in Vorgrimler: 127-134

[30]   Erhueh, *Image of God in Man*, p.179ff.

[31]   Cf. Augustine, *Civ. Dei.* 13.14. It is also the other aspect of solidarity with Adam and with Christ. The notion of solidarity is critical to an effective understanding of the work of Christ. This Augustinian sense is to the fore in GS 14.

who is the True and the Good.   Effectively, therefore, atheism destroys the interior freedom of the person which is dependent upon this orientation to God - here conscience comes into play - and further erodes human solidarity.[32]   One way of appreciating the contemporary significance of the Constitution's understanding of *interioritas* is to see it as the expression of the ontological groundedness or "depth" of the human person.   In this respect, *interioritas* becomes an interesting point of engagement with Postmodernity and its flight from ontology into surfaces and the transitory performative self.[33]

It is this ontological depth that is, I believe, at the heart of the Constitution's treatment of "sin".   There is always in Christianity a realism about the wounded nature of humanity and society.   This is why existence in all its modalities is a drama; not only because of the historical instability of human choices, knowledge and freedom, but because of the deeper reality of sin.   Such instability is grounded at the very level of being itself.   In its fundamental goodness and plasticity, the potentialities of being are all placed in jeopardy because of a disordered human freedom.   The risk lies in the paradox at the heart of human nature that informs our self-understanding. Shakespeare's Lear, in a moment of self-confrontation, speaks out of a broken existential madness: "Thou art the thing itself, unaccommodated man is no more but such a

---

[32]   In a positive sense, *interioritas* is seen as the condition for building up culture cf. GS 58.

[33]   For a useful way into this discussion cf. Schrag, C. O., *The Self after Postmodernity* (USA, Yale University Press, 1997). Especially where he attempts to develop the notion of the self 'in transcendence' but strangely misses the Augustinian and Catholic tradition.   For the necessity of the interior life for a reflective moral life, cf. Murdoch, I., *The Sovereignty of The Good* (London (1970), Routledge PK, 1989).   Also Charles Taylor's discussion of interiority in *Sources of the Self* (Cambridge, Cambridge University Press, 1989), pp. 127 ff.

poor bare, forked animal as thou art ..." Alexander Pope expresses the moment more coolly: "Great Lord of all things, yet a prey to all, Sole judge of truth, in endless error hurl'd, The glory, jest and riddle of the world". [34]

This paradox is not primarily the result of our fragile existence in an elemental world largely indifferent to us and our history. It arises because our existence is one that is self-aware, grounded in our *interioritas*, our search in a world for understanding and meaning. But the search is already occluded because of our instability. Christ reveals to us that this instability does not reside primarily in our finitude - for that is not an obstacle for an incarnate God - but in our sinfulness. Sin, as such, is not simply a moral failure but an epistemological one; it touches on the foundations of our being, for it alienates us from our own being and truth. Our search, therefore, is not frustrated because of a silent cosmos, or even by a silent God; it is frustrated by the paradox that we are to ourselves: human existence is "agonistic". *Gaudium et spes* captures this drama in the language of Pascal's "grandeur and misery" and many have observed its tension between a Teilhardian optimism and a Pascalian pessimism.[35] However, rather than seeing this as a tension between two schools that have not been fully reconciled, I think it is more productive to understand it as the tension proper to the soteriological drama of history or, in the words of

---

[34]   Cf. GS 13; 21. Also Pascal who develops the similar theme of the paradox but sees knowledge of our sin as intrinsic to self-knowledge. *Pensées*, §131, (ET by A.J. Krailsheimer, London, Penguin Classics 1995).

[35]   Cf. Ratzinger, J. 'The Dignity Of The Human Person' in Vorgrimler: p. 128, Dupré, L., *Passage to Modernity* (New Haven, Yale University Press, 1993). Also Duffy, S., *The Graced Horizon* (Collegeville, MN. Liturgical Press, 1992). This is a very good survey and discussion of the debates in the contemporary theology of nature and grace in the Catholic tradition.

Maurice Blondel, the "divine drama" which is the action of grace in every soul.[36]

It is important not to miss the significant way in which the Constitution understands this and seeks to develop a dynamic soteriology of culture, which is, of course, God's presence in the world. In this soteriology the sacred and the secular are distinct but are ordered to each other and, indeed, neither can come to a full actualisation without the other. It is this integral vision that determines the Church's mission in the world and allows her to exist within every culture without seeking to impose a specific form that could only be culturally and historically conditioned. So, the Constitution struggles to conceptualise the actual salvific relationship as well as the theoretical one between the universal destiny of humanity and the particular expression this must take in any given time, place, or culture. It is a Christological co-ordination that draws from the doctrine of grace that informs the whole of the Conciliar vision. At its centre is a refusal to allow the "no" of sin to be greater than God's creative mercy in Christ, while never minimising the depth of the "no" and what it puts at risk. Here, I believe, the conceptualisation is fundamentally Augustinian before it is Teilhardian or Pascalian. It is worth exploring this a little.

The dispute between Augustine and Pelagius is not simply about the moral perfectibility of the human person - our capacity to be educated, so to speak.[37] It is a

---

[36]   Blondel, M. 'Lettre sur L'Apologétique' in *Les premiers écrits de Maurice Blondel* II (Paris, 1956), pp.88-89. Given that Blondel is the inspiration behind the whole approach of the *nouvelle théologie*, it can be no accident that the category of drama emerges as a key way of understanding God's intimate engagement with the world.
[37]   For a contrast between Augustine and the Greek Fathers on this and its relation to the Pelagian debate cf. Ladner, G. B., "St Augustine's Conception Of The Reformation Of Man To The Image Of God", in *Augustinus Magister, Congrés International Augustinien*, 1954 (Communications Paris, Études Augustiniennes, 1954).

difference about the radical nature of salvation and the work of Christ: for Augustine, Christ is no moral Magister but an ontological Doctor - a healer of being.[38] We may not agree with every aspect of his formulation of the radical consequences of sin, but his insight that sin is not just a moral problem but an ontological one is surely correct: if we do not know who we are, how can we know what to do? Without knowing who we are, the very intelligibility of our actions and their purpose is called into question. There is in Augustine an intimate connection between goodness and holiness - in a sense holiness is the perfection of goodness. We have already encountered this theme in *Gaudium et spes*. We are called ultimately to participate in the communicative transcendence of goodness that is perfected in holiness, thereby sanctifying God's good creation in the righteousness which flows from a justified and sanctified human actor. Life is not just about acting in goodness and truth but being good and true; we cannot do one without the other and *vice versa*. It is, literally, a question of our integrity. As such, it is a matter of life and death.[39] Sin, especially foundational or original sin, obstructs and diverts this movement; it therefore makes us ontological vulnerable. This is why the Catholic understanding will always be uncomfortable with a Protestant *simul iustus et peccator*.

The "agonistics" of our existence is not because the world itself is bad - the Manichean position is always rejected - but because "I" don't know how to live in it - and therefore don't know how to 'be' in it. Given the reciprocal relationship we touched on in *interioritas*, I risk misusing the world and therefore put it and myself at risk.

---

[38] For a treatment of the theme of 'Christus Medicus' in Augustine cf. Arbesmann, R., "The Concept Of Christus Medicus In Augustine", in *Traditio*, Vol. 10, 1954. Cf also Argimiro Turrado, *Dios en el Hombre, Plenitud o tragedia* (Madrid, BAC 1971), pp. 224-228.
[39] GS 13.

Human sinfulness is a sort of "un-making" of God's creative making - sin brings with it an ontological risk. If, therefore, we are to understand correctly our actions in the world, we must understand the dynamics of sin in us and how that wounds and disrupts the world, disrupting its own integrity, and breaking the community of all created things; robbing them of their goodness by obstructing their potential ordering in holiness.[40] Grace is the restoration of our "Integrity" our "communion" not just with God but with humanity and the world in which we live. At its most profound, grace is a healing of being and gives us again the possibility of becoming "real" - it is our "humanisation". This is the work of Christ, who discloses within history and cultures what it is to be human and with that the purpose of human activity in the world. For this reason it is important to understand the significance of the theology set out in Part I of *Gaudium et spes*. Without it we misunderstand Part II: it is not the sketch of a political or cultural programme for human betterment, but a description of the way in which the world is healed through a healed humanity: mission and soteriology, action and being, are not to be separated so that the community of creation, at all levels, can move under God's grace to its realization.

Gaudium et spes has rejected a purely Cartesian account of what it is to be human and with it a modern individualism. It indicates how our actions in the world can be a real act of consecration of ourselves and the world, therefore an effective realisation of the priestly character of Christians and, implicitly, of all humanity that

---

[40] The theological foundation of Part I in *Gaudium et spes* is clearly significant for Part II when seen in this way. Thus the internal ordering of society and the international ordering of nations in peace and human flourishing is not just a moral question but an ontological one. Although *Gaudium et spes* does not deal directly with contemporary concerns about the environment it provides an important way into the question and anticipates what will be developed into an understanding of 'structural sin'.

bears the image of Christ who is priest. Human cultures, at the national and international levels, are human artefacts. As such they reflect the human "soul" as well as the material needs and forces that shape society. Culture can nourish the soul or it can wound and impoverish it. It can also express and mediate grace; this is why it needs to be sanctified.[41]

Although we have compressed a complex and rich theology into a few paragraphs, it is possible to see how, although *Gaudium et spes* has Christology as its explicit theme, it develops and applies it in terms of a pneumatology.[42] It is to this that we now turn.

The Work of the Holy Spirit

The famous opening words of the Constitution, from which it receives its title, already mark it in terms of the gifts of the Spirit: joy and hope - the gifts of consolation, set in opposition to those of desolation. The drama of human existence which we have been exploring is also the drama of the Spirit within history, bringing about the kingdom of Christ. It has become common to criticize the great documents of the Council for their optimism. It is not often appreciated, however, that this is not a naïve optimism but one that reflects this outpouring and activity of the Holy Spirit. Such a vision is deeply embedded in *Gaudium et spes*: the recovery of the world is part of the saving work of Christ; it comes through our participation in his work, and that participation is the activity of the Holy Spirit. As noted by Heribut Mühlen, the Council goes beyond a "pre-

---

[41]   Cf. Here John Paul II's letter to artists (1999) on the "epiphany of beauty", as an occasion or expression of the encounter with grace, draws upon Paul VI's address to artists on a similar occasion (1967)

[42]   GS 22. Which echoes Pascal, "Let us learn our true nature from the uncreated and incarnate truth', *Pensées*, (ET. by A.J. Krailsheimer, London, Penguin Classics, 1995), §131.

trinitarian monotheism". This is clearly seen in *Lumen gentium*, but it also makes *Gaudium et spes* possible. As we have seen, it may be argued that more than any of the other documents of the Council, it begins to develop a pneumatology.[43]

Here especially we see how closely *Gaudium et spes* is connected to *Lumen gentium*. *Gaudium et spes* takes the themes of mystery and of holiness developed in their ecclesiological context by *Lumen gentium*, and expands them into concrete cultural, social, and international realms. This really constitutes a systematic reflection on the mission of the Church as the presence and sign of the Kingdom of God. Behind it lies a significant tradition of theological thought, extending from the Fathers through the great scholastic thinkers, which understands the Beatitudes in terms of the gifts of the Holy Spirit.[44] Such gifts are not only personal but social;

---

[43]   Cf.Mühlen, H. *L'Esprit dans l'Eglise* (Paris, 1969) for an extensive treatment. Kärkkäinen, Veli-Matti, *Pneumatology, The Holy Spirit in Ecumenical, International and Contextual Perspective*, pp. 74-79 has a wholly inadequate and superficial treatment. It is a major defect in Rowland that she fails to attend to the pneumatology of *Gaudium et spes*.

[44]   The tradition is represented in Aquinas' treatment of the gifts of the Holy Spirit that are ordered to overcome our natural knowledge. Cf.Summa Ia-IIae q.68-70   In his treatment Aquinas establishes the theology of the spiritual life. The Beatitudes and the Gifts are organised around a threefold division of the life of pleasure, action and contemplation. The forth and fifth Beatitudes - Blessed are those that hunger and thirst for justice or righteousness and those that are merciful - are concerned with the active life. For an influential commentary on Aquinas' teaching on the Holy Spirit, cf. John of St Thomas, *Treatise on The Gifts of the Holy Spirit* ; cf. especially chapter 9, 'The Beatitudes and Fruits' (ET. Dominic Hughes O.P., *The Gifts of the Holy Spirit*, London, Sheed and Ward, 1951). Gardeil's treatment in the *Dictionnaire de Théologie Catholique* (1911) and his *Les dons du Sant-Ésprit dans les saints dominicans* (Paris, 1903), but especially his *Le Saint-Esprit dans la vie chrétienne* (Paris, Les Éditions du Cerf, 1925). Congar also has a brief but illuminating

they have a communitarian dimension. To some extent this is combined with a Trinitarian understanding of communion or *koinonia* - the work of the Spirit who is the bond of love. If Christ is the formal principle that guides the thought of *Gaudium et spes*, the material principle is love, the perfection of all the virtues, realised in the gift of the Holy Spirit. This can be seen in the extraordinary paragraph 22: "This applies not only to Christians but to all people of goodwill in whose hearts grace is secretly at work. Since Christ died for everyone, and since the ultimate calling of each of us comes from God and is therefore a universal one, we are obliged to hold that the Holy Spirit offers everyone the possibility of sharing in this paschal mystery in a manner known to God".

Pneumatology lies at the heart of soteriology. *Gaudium et spes* begins to sketch the implications of this in terms of the way in which the grace of Christ is offered in and through social and cultural structures which seek to express the dignity of humanity and the common vocation of all grounded in the *imago Dei*.

When we begin to understand the way in which God offers his grace to all as the mission of the Spirit, then we can see how truly and completely God is at work in this world and we are at home in it. In his poem *Birches*, Robert Frost unwittingly captures this, "Earth's the right place for love: I don't know where it's likely to go better". The Incarnation guarantees this truth. *Gaudium et spes* in calling us to live it, assures us that we can and that we do.

---

treatment, in *I Believe in the Holy Spirit, Vol. II*. (ET David Smith, London, Chapman, 1983: 134-141).

BROADCASTING AND THE IDEA OF THE PUBLIC

Mark Thompson, Director-General of the BBC, points to a similarity between the Church in the modern world, as described in *Gaudium et spes*, and the mission of the BBC. Both find their responsibilities to a global public demand that they preserve a generous, open and objective public forum. This poses serious challenges in a "public space" teeming with a plurality of views.

Recently, the Archbishop of Canterbury gave a speech about journalism. Called *The Media: Public Interest and Common Good*, it examined the notion of the "public interest" - which is frequently cited by journalists to justify investigations and revelations which otherwise might be regarded as intrusive and destructive - and concluded that, although the best journalism really does support the common good and the interests of a "mature democracy", some aspects of what some British journalists do are, to use his words, "lethally damaging" to the reputation of contemporary journalism and "contribute to the embarrassingly low level of trust in the profession (especially in the UK) shown in most opinion polls."

Predictably the immediate response to the speech was a good deal of huffing and puffing by columnists and leader-writers. Wasn't this a classic example of a defensive establishment figure moaning about a noisy, unruly but essentially healthy free press? Didn't Archbishop Rowan's speech blur two fundamentally different things: the prurient invasion of the private lives of individuals by the tabloids, and the robust challenging of people and institutions necessarily in the public sphere, with public duties and accountabilities?

I don't want to enter directly into this debate, except to note that the Archbishop was surely right to point out that, as the old saw has it, not everything that interests the public is in the public interest, and that - and I speak, God help me, as a journalist myself - it is difficult to think of any other trade, with the possible exception of the law, which is more enthusiastic than journalism about dishing out criticism to others or more touchy about receiving it itself.

But there was something the Archbishop said which sent my mind off in a slightly different direction, one which follows the idea of the public or publicness, and which - to me at least - connects this idea both with what we try to do at the BBC and with some of the central themes of *Gaudium et spes*. And if I'm right, following this route takes us to some interesting questions about the future.

A Necessary Fiction?

Let's begin with what Archbishop Rowan said:

> "A public is a necessary fiction. If a journalist or broadcaster, or of course, rather more significantly, a proprietor wants to secure consumers, a sense of solidarity and loyalty has to be built up; and it is built up very effectively by two complementary strategies. One is to communicate as if every reader or consumer shared the same fundamental values and preferences and anxieties. The other is to communicate as if these fundamental values and so on were the natural moral world of everyone with a brain or a conscience. The calculation of what will surprise (or better still, shock) the public is based on a careful assessment of what is unassailable and utterly taken for granted by that public... The public is assumed to be homogeneous; and this particular public is assumed to be representative of the real moral life of society."

In other words, a media magnate - a Citizen Kane, or perhaps a Citizen Murdoch, if you like - creates a model of the public, idealised or exaggerated or perhaps merely averaged from focus-groups and surveys, and addresses every real reader or viewer both as if they were a perfect example of this model and as if the model itself represented some kind of peak of understanding and moral rectitude. Readers or viewers are assured that they are both like-minded and right-minded; but the whole thing is a projection, an imprecise and commercially-motivated exercise in market segmentation rather than a genuine meeting of minds.

Now reading this, two lateral thoughts occurred to me. The first rather unexpected one is that, if you think about it, the two strategies the Archbishop mentions - to communicate as if everyone you are talking to shares the same fundamental values and as if these fundamental values represent a common natural moral world - are strategies we normally associate with organised religion rather than with the media. Christianity and Islam in particular have historically tended to present themselves to believers and nonbelievers alike in just these terms. Are we to see the modern media in some way then as a rival to traditional religion, each outlet projecting its own claim to moral universality - a claim based not of course on revelation but on the science of marketing? Or should we look the other way at religion itself?

Although perfect model *Daily Mail* or *Guardian* readers probably do exist, most of us frequently find ourselves dissenting to some degree from opinions expressed in those and other newspapers which are presented as self-evident - we discover that we are not perfect members of that particular public after all. We find that our sense of identity, our relationship with the newspaper is a provisional one. And wise editors and proprietors are aware of this. They hire columnists with views that oppose the majority view of the paper, they allow a certain elasticity of tone and opinion. Their projection of the public is rather more nuanced and negotiated than it first appears. But can institutions or bodies of believers who are certain that they are in possession of absolute and definitive truths about God and human morality negotiate in this way? How do they communicate with nonbelievers and partial believers - with, if you like, the shaded areas around their projected public? That question seems to me to be one of the starting points of *Gaudium et spes*.

But the sentence that most struck me in that passage was that first arresting one: "a public is a necessary fiction". It is probably true in the case of newspapers and political parties and most other apparently public communities and associations. But is it always true?

The BBC and the Public

Well, interestingly, it is not true of the BBC. Indeed, I'd go further: for the BBC, the public is not a necessary fiction, it is a necessary fact. There is a real public as well as a multiplicity of projected ones and, if we ever lose sight of it or of the concept of publicness, there will certainly be no further need for a BBC. The point I am making is not in any sense a rhetorical one. 96% of the UK population use our services every month. 94% pay a licence-fee. To all intents and purposes, everyone uses the BBC and everyone pays for it.

Our public then is not white or black, not prosperous or poor, not Christian or non-Christian, not materialist or otherworldly, not progressive or traditionalist, but all these things all at once. It's everybody: our universality is literal. Now of course a given programme - Colin and Edie on Radio 1, an

59

investigative documentary on BBC2 - might well think of a particular core audience with a certain set of shared attitudes and tastes, but much of what we do reaches very large audience aggregates indeed and, taken together, our services try to address every age group, every socio-economic demographic and every geographical part of the UK as well as many hundreds of millions of people around the world.

So we have a real public. But the concept of publicness runs deeper than usage. Rowan Williams talked rightly about the "marketising" of the media and the consequent tendency for content to be commoditised. But again, in a literal rather than rhetorical sense, the public service BBC does not operate in a market, nor does it have consumers. Because it is founded on the principle of pooled investment, the BBC as currently constituted does not compete in the selling of commercial impacts to advertisers or of subscriptions. As I learned when I was Chief Executive of Channel 4, advertisers value some viewers far more than others - an affluent young woman in the 16-34 demographic has eyeballs which are worth many multiples of those of a pensioner of limited means - and this differential inevitably skews creative decisions. Broadcasters like BSkyB, whose business model is based on subscription, again are incentivised to provide services which appeal to high-spending households. But to the BBC, everyone - no matter what their age or income - has the same value.

Broadcasting - by which I mean universal free-to-air broadcasting - is, like architecture, a civic art. It is intrinsically public both in ambition and in effect. It is a public space into which anyone and everyone is free to come and roam. And again it's worth noting the effect of an economic model in which people do not pay at the point of use. Turning on the TV or radio or wandering through our pages on the internet does not involve an economic choice on the part of the user. The goods we provide, moreover, are to all intents and purposes what economists call public goods - they do not get consumed by one person so that they cannot be enjoyed by the next. The people who use the BBC's services, in other words, do not behave like consumers and nothing gets consumed. In theory then, the BBC stands almost wholly outside the rather troubling picture which the Archbishop drew of contemporary media. In practice, of course, things are a little more complicated.

First, the BBC does not exist in splendid isolation. We're part of a wider media environment. Many of our producers and journalists have been recruited from other media organisations. We compete for stories and ideas with our commercial counterparts. Inevitably our editors absorb and take note of the way in which the big issues of the day are being covered with others.

Much of this influence is positive. Competition - including commercial competition - is good for us and our audiences. Diversity of analysis and viewpoint makes all good journalists stop and reconsider their own preconceptions. Journalistic teams of diverse experience and from diverse backgrounds thicken the creative plot for us and our audiences. And, I should add, I don't think a day goes by when - despite all the pressures and problems which Rowan Williams refers to - we can't learn something of value from the professionalism and talent of our commercial colleagues.

But there are real things to worry about too. Impartiality and objectivity are becoming rarer qualities in mainstream journalism. Historical knowledge - especially of complex international stories like Israel/Palestine - can no longer be assumed. 24 hour news services mean that the public can get their news pretty much when and where they like, but they can put a terrible strain on the time needed for reflection and judgement. Presumption of bad faith and what used rather grandly to be called a hermeneutics of suspicion do seem to be becoming more widespread.

Now it would be possible to wring one's hands and blame the zeitgeist, but over the past year at the BBC, we've tried to take some practical steps to address these concerns. In the aftermath of the Gilligan-Kelly-Hutton affair, we've strengthened many of our internal journalistic safeguards. We've put literally thousands of our journalists through new training courses in which issues of fair-mindedness, and our absolute duty to give those against whom we make serious allegations the right to reply take centre stage. We plan to create a virtual 'college of journalism' to promote the knowledge and values on which the editors and correspondents of the future can rely. We've appointed new editors - for example, for Europe and Middle East - to ensure consistency and depth in our coverage. We've published new editorial guidelines for every producer and content creator in the BBC. Privacy and the particular challenge of balancing public interest arguments against the right of everyone not to be subjected to unwarranted intrusion feature heavily.

A Question of Values

All this is as it should be and I could touch on other aspects of what the BBC does - its commitment to learning, for instance, or to creativity and cultural life - and tell a similar story of opportunities and pressures and plans.

But there's a larger question at stake, which is this: if we accept the idea of this larger, truer public and the civic space it occupies, what, if any, values can we predicate of it? Given its almost limitless diversity, do we

62

not run the risk of re-fictionalising it, as it were, if we attempt to project any given set of meaningful values on it? Individuals in the crowd may well have strong and coherent values, perhaps ones we share ourselves, but these values may be contradicted by other, equally strong views held by their neighbours or by people in another part of the square.

This may sound like a problem calling for a moral philosopher or a theologian, but again - and pretty much uniquely - it's an immediate and day-to-day issue for the BBC. Let me give you a couple of examples.

Pluralism and openness are vital for a broadcaster who attempts to address every individual and every community in society. Different belief-systems, different religious and aesthetic attitudes, different perspectives on what is and isn't acceptable in terms of taste and decency, in fact pretty much every boundary of difference will be explored and tested. Even if one refuses to accept any kind of absolute set of human values, there are clearly limits around what we could call majority acceptance and majority tolerance. But - particularly as the perspectives of old and young continue to diverge, especially around taste and decency - some of those limits are becoming progressively more contested.

In 2004, after much reflection, we decided not to show the animated comedy *Popetown*. As a result, many commentators, especially those who seem to have a humanist or anti-religious agenda, concluded that we were bowing in a rather craven way to pressure from the religious lobby. A few weeks later, after at least as much reflection, we decided to show a televised version of *Jerry Springer The Opera*. Now a different group of commentators tried to convince the world that the BBC had finally taken off its mask and revealed itself as the arch-secularist they'd always suspected it to be. Move on three months and the Corporation was devoting what was to some a suspicious amount of time and coverage to the death of one pope and the election of another. I don't know what conspiracy-theorists made of our BBC2 programme *The Monastery*, a diabolical mixture of reality TV and the rule of St Benedict set here at Worth - but I can report that on one of its showings it comfortably beat *Celebrity Love Island* over on ITV. Habit beats bikini shock.

The point is this. Any one of these decisions can be taken to be evidence of some underlying agenda - a covert or semi-covert attempt to convert the public to some particular world-view. Taken together, they either reveal a plot worthy of *The Da Vinci Code* - you may not want to rule that out, by the way - or an organisation trying to make a series of rational decisions, each on its own merits, while taking incoming fire from both sets of trenches in what has become a shooting-war about religion, taste and free speech. Maintaining an open creative space in which diversity can thrive and around which there are sensible, coherent boundaries turns out to be slightly harder than it looks.

Let's take a second example - our coverage of the *Live 8* concerts in Hyde Park and other cities around the world. The Make Poverty History campaign can pose very different editorial challenges for the BBC than *Popetown* or Jerry Springer. It has broad cross-party support and, it seems, overwhelming public backing. Scepticism, perhaps even opposition exists but is muted - if there is a Please Keep Poverty Going party, it's decided to keep its head down for the moment.

Nonetheless, our own values, in particular our sense of our responsibility always to try to offer audiences objectivity and context, meant that - although many, many of my colleagues I'm sure supported the objectives of *Live*

8 wholeheartedly - we couldn't simply join the bandwagon. It wasn't a day for impersonal, dispassionate impartiality - and anyone who watched Jonathan Ross will know that we certainly weren't purveying that - but we did try hard to get a range of voices in. *The Mail On Sunday* had great fun with a list of ten guidelines - or "commandments" as they inevitably dubbed them - which we'd issued before the event. Here's a sample: "the BBC cannot present one solution to world poverty". And that's true - it's our job to reflect the wider public mood, to allow people at home to celebrate and share in great moments of common experience and empathy, but it's also our job to carry on finding space for the awkward questions too.

We've presented a major season of programmes about Africa, many of them on peak-time BBC1. The joy and the hope - those resonant words - of *Live 8* was a fitting part, and an emotional climax to that season. But so too was Fergal Keane's sombre *Panorama* from Darfur a day later. In the world of Rowan Williams' fictional public, it's tempting for media proprietor and public to collude, to stick to the comfortable and the popular. Sometimes it's the BBC's role to break the spell.

Live 8 was a great success and an amazing achievement by Bob Geldof, Richard Curtis and many others. We were proud to bring it to many millions of people in this country and perhaps two billion people around the world. But I'm also proud that, uncomfortable though it sometimes was, we remembered that it was an important part of the story, not the whole story.

Engaging with an Open Society

But the dilemmas I've talked about arise not because the public space in which the BBC operates is value-free; but because it is teeming with values, many of them passionately held. One often hears people inveighing against the amorality of contemporary society. It's true, as I've suggested, that some moral standards which were once widely accepted, are now disputed and that we bump into many of these disputes in broadcasting: the use of foul language, the limits of secular propriety, the respect due to organised religion and so on. If you define public morality entirely around these issues and take a traditional view on all of them, then you may well believe that we are living through a period of moral degradation.

But it would have been hard to walk through the *Live 8* crowds, or watch news pictures of the Edinburgh march; to witness the public response to the tsunami at the start of 2005r or to *Comic Relief* a few months later; to see the interest and respect with which our audiences marked the passing of John Paul II - hard to see any of these things and conclude that the public at large holds no moral concerns in common.

I asked a few minutes ago what values we could predicate of my maximal definition of the public. Despite the areas of contention, I believe that the list of values held by an overwhelming majority of people is a long one: respect for the common law; a concern for the protection of the vulnerable and the disadvantaged; a strong sense of natural justice and fair play; a hunger for honesty and the truth; an empathy with suffering; an acknowledgement of the centrality of human dignity. And I haven't plucked this list out of the air - all of these values are visible in the public's reaction to what we broadcast, the judgements they make about individual programmes and editorial judgements, the thousands of letters and e-mails I receive. For the majority of our audience, the public space we broadcast into is also a moral space.

The emphasis and expression of the values may change - as programmes like Big Brother famously show, many viewers today clearly take a broader view of what personal human dignity consists of than would have been the case a generation ago - but it is not obvious that these sets of values are in aggregate decline. As the events of this week have shown, collective concern about global poverty seems to be on the rise, to take only one example.

Two Anthropologies

If we go back to where I began with Rowan William's definition of the small public, the convenient public of the media proprietor, and compare it to this second, maximal public, it's as if one is considering two rival anthropologies: the first narrow, explicit, instrumental; the second expansive and inclusive. Values in the first are clear and uniform but also in some sense imposed, top-down; values in the second are uneven and at the margins disputed but also seem to spring naturally from a sense of what human beings are capable of. This second anthropology, in other words, is less ordered than the first but also more positive in its orientation, more optimistic even.

And this for me is precisely where *Gaudium et spes* comes in. Because to me - and I speak, I should say without being encumbered by a single ounce of theological knowledge - the issue which the Constitution deals with is exactly the 'maximal public' which I have been describing and the way in which the Church should engage with it and interact with it:

> "The world the Council has in mind then is the world of men, the entire human family, its whole environment; the world which is the theatre of human history, marked with man's industry, his triumphs and disasters" [GS 2].

There is a new and fresh sense - a "grateful appreciation" [GS 44] - of how the Church itself benefits from its location in the heart of the wider human environment and a remarkably strong statement of the value of openness and freedom in society:

Culture springs from the rational and social nature of man continually; therefore it needs proper liberty to develop itself and scope to operate autonomously. Quite rightly then it commands respect and is in a certain sense inviolable, saving the rights of persons and the community and within the limits of the common good.

The Council declares that "there are two distinct orders of knowledge" [GS 59], that of faith and that of reason, and that the Church plainly does not forbid that "human learning and arts...should use their own principles and methods in their own fields" [GS 59]. In other words, "recognising this just liberty" [GS 59], she affirms the rightful autonomy of human culture and "especially of the sciences" [GS 59].

Gaudium et spes pictures the Church not as a separate 'small' public, a projected 'we' defined at least in part by its rejection of other cultures, but as a community in continual dialogue with the largest human community that can be imagined. Although it is utterly clear about the Church's unique mission and unique claim to the truth, it sees engagement with the world not as a struggle for separation or for victory but as a kind of affirmative dialectic. And it understands that this dialectic is only possible if the openness of society, "this just liberty", this "rightful autonomy of human culture" is maintained.

It also does not confuse pluralism with relativism. In the years since *Gaudium et spes* was written, some have wondered whether what Cardinal Scola calls in his introduction to the latest edition this "changed attitude to the contemporary world" didn't represent a kind of selling of the pass. But I believe that's wrong. In an open society, defective, even wicked ideas may be expressed or promoted, but there's a big difference between respecting people's right to say or believe what they want to, and feeling that you have to give every view an equal status, or somehow agree with everyone at the same time. And it's dangerous to blur proper opposition to the false and negative beliefs which an open society permits with opposition to the virtue of openness itself.

Consider rather the role Jonathan Sachs, the Chief Rabbi, assigns to the idea of conversation in his book *The Dignity of Difference*:

> "In a debate one side wins, the other loses but both are the same as they were before. In a conversation neither side loses and both are changed, because they now know what reality looks like from a different perspective. This is not to say that either side gives up its previous convictions. That is not what conversation is about. In a plural society - all the more so in a plural world - each of us has to settle for less than we do when we associate with fellow believers. Yet what we lose is more than compensated for by the fact that together we are co-architects of a society larger than we could construct on our own. Society is a conversation scored for many voices. But it is precisely in and through that conversation that we become conjoint authors of our collective future."

This notion of the bigger conversation, a conversation which does not dilute or vitiate belief but which enriches it, seems to me to be at the heart of *Gaudium et spes*. And it's difficult to read the Gospels, isn't it, without believing that our religion began as a conversation - a conversation in the street or around the dinner table, a conversation between believers and nonbelievers, a conversation from which no-one was excluded.

The Future of 'Publicness'

Perhaps I could end with a few thoughts about the future of what I've called public space or the idea of a universal public. In his book *The Open Society and its Enemies*, Karl Popper identified classical Athens as the first society which could be described as open. He also identified its first opponents - Critias and Plato - men who believed that openness would lead inevitably to anarchy and social collapse and that the only solution was a return to a closed, effectively tribal society. Again, I think we can see Plato's *Republic* as yet another projection of a 'small public', tightly defined and tightly controlled with freedom and inclusion sacrificed as the price for security.

Every age - and every institution - probably has its Platos, but I think we stand right now at an interesting point in the endless dynamic between the open and the closed, and at least from where I'm sitting the forces ranged on both sides seem formidable.

Publicness is under attack and from a number of different directions. Probably the greatest threat the BBC itself faces is from a group of economists - not all economists, by the way, perhaps not even a majority, but an influential group nonetheless - who have an 'in-principle' objection to the idea of free-to-air broadcasting, especially if paid for by a compulsory licence-fee. As soon as technology allows, they would rather move to a world where consumers purchased audio-visual content in the way they purchase other goods, one transaction at a time. This part of public space - and I believe that broadcasting is one of the most important parts of all public space - would become private.

But there are other threats too. Extremists are getting adept at using the new technologies not just to make their case legitimately but to threaten. The campaign against the broadcast of *Jerry Springer* was internet and e-mail driven. Nothing wrong in that of course, and I have to say that the overwhelming majority of e-mails we received were courteous and thoughtful. But the internet allowed the group *Christian Voice* to post the names, phone numbers and private addresses of some of my colleagues. As a result - though I accept it may well not have been *Christian Voice's* intention - there were a number of threats of violence against them and their families. Most days in the news, not just here but around the world, there are examples of technology and the vulnerabilities of open, democratic societies being exploited by the intolerant.

But there is another, quite different side to the story. As our coverage of *Live 8* and the meeting of G8 leaders in Gleneagles shows, technology is also an extraordinarily powerful force in joining humanity together, of creating a public space which is little short of global. And, although people worry endlessly and properly about the dangers of cyberspace, or how untrammelled freedom of communication and association can be abused, it seems to me that these technologies are finally both liberating and empowering: it is no accident that repressive societies regard the internet as a profoundly dangerous and subversive development. In its own way, moreover, the internet has reinforced that idea of public space as free space, or more precisely space which is not fully marketised, where you can wander and look and converse without every action becoming a transaction.

Forty years on, *Gaudium et spes* seems far-sighted in its intuition of the coming of this world and in its hope not just for the Church but for the whole of humanity. It recognises in a striking and fresh way that human liberty and plurality support rather than hinder the Church's own mission in the world and emphasises a view of humanity which is fully continuous with its own understanding of the unique and definitive climax of God's self-communication in the Incarnation. It calls for human institutions to be "gradually brought into harmony with spiritual purposes" [GS 29], though it adds rather wistfully (and very possibly with the BBC in mind), "this may take a long time" [GS 29]. That is no doubt right, though I would argue that it is the Constitution's simultaneous awareness of the magnitude of the task and the possibility of the task that lends it force and credibility. And it points to a specifically Christian anthropology - one which recognises that Christians themselves, to quote Karl Rahner, "have not known enough, or loved enough, or suffered enough," but that they share a nature with the rest of mankind that with God's grace is capable of anything.

Now, not everyone accepts the faith in which that optimism is grounded, but the optimism itself is something to share and build on, part of the wider challenge of connecting and engaging humanity, in which secular institutions like the BBC have a role to play, alongside the central role which the Church sees for herself in leading that conversation, which excludes no-one, which can deepen, and fortifies, and which will never end.

WHERE IS THE CHURCH IN THE MODERN WORLD?

Professor Nicholas Boyle presents a case for the *contemporary* worth of *Gaudium et spes* and the relation between the account of Modernity it offers and a properly Christian hope. He then asks what reason the Church can give for living and hoping in the modern European Union.

There has long been a whispering campaign against *Gaudium et spes*. The right view these days, the grapevine hints, is that the Vatican Council's most impressively systematic document, the *Pastoral Constitution on the Church in the Modern World*, was really an afterthought, a placatory gesture towards 1960s liberalism. It was Pelagian, it was impossibly optimistic about human progress, it added nothing significant to the Council's other documents, and above all it was dated: nothing fades so quickly as notions of what is modern. None of these charges sticks, as we shall see, but the last is the most facile. In GS 91 the Fathers themselves admit that their "programme will have to be further pursued and amplified, since it often deals with matters in a constant state of development." Yet my principal impression on reading the Constitution in 2005 is how little that expected development has changed the analysis and the "programme" itself. The short answer to the question: where is the Church in the Modern World? is: wherever the modern world finds that it must express its own nature and purpose in the terms provided for it by *Gaudium et spes*. *Gaudium et spes* is a deeply courageous and missionary document. It knows that the Church's founding commission is to go out and teach all nations, and that a Church that has grown timorous and fearful for its future serves no purpose at all. Such a Church would be like the man in the parable who feared the authority of his Lord and wrapped up his talent in a napkin in case he lost it. *Gaudium et spes* also knows that you can teach only those whom you are willing to understand and that you can understand only those whose position you are willing to share. The colossal potential God has given to a world of six billion human persons, mostly young, needs to be understood and affirmed if it is to be directed towards the goal that God intends for it.

In this lecture I want to do two things. After a brief word about the charge of datedness, I shall consider the relation between the account of modernity offered by *Gaudium et spes* and a properly Christian hope. Then I shall consider the specific case of Europe: what reasons can the Church give for living and hoping in the modern, expanded - perhaps still further to be expanded - European Union?

First, then, it is true that, like any piece of effective thinking, and like all the Church's authoritative documents, from the very earliest, *Gaudium et spes* bears the marks of the time in which it was composed. Its most obviously dated stylistic feature is largely, though not entirely, a fault of the English translators: its insistently masculinist vocabulary. 'Man' recurs in every other line in the early sections, as of course he did in the 1960s when people wanted to be taken seriously: Neil Armstrong's carefully drafted words on landing on the Moon were the most public culmination of a thoughtlessly chauvinist rhetoric of humanism which it was one of the great achievements of 1970s feminism to render unusable. In secular discourse, we don't talk about 'Man' in a high moral tone any more, and that I think is a good thing, and not just for reasons of gender politics. Then again, it cannot be denied that *Gaudium et spes* shows itself a document of the period from 1949 to 1989 in its numerous references to, for example, "the ambition to propagate one's own ideology" [GS 8], "opposing camps" [GS 82], or "some state

74

authorities" that "promote atheism" [GS 21, 20]. However, only historical exegesis will now tell us that these are allusions to the great stand-off between the USA and the USSR that dominated 'modern' minds in the mid-twentieth century. Like other period features of the document's style, they play no deeper role in the analysis. In 1965 this indeterminacy of language looked like evasiveness, a mealy-mouthed refusal to name names in the battle of those paper tigers, Capitalism and Communism. We can now see how shrewd the Council was not to allow such terms to structure what it had to say about modernity. Instead, and remarkably, for a philosophical and theological statement prepared amid all the public illusions and deceptions of the height of the Cold War, *Gaudium et spes* offers a definition of what makes the modern world modern that is bang up-to-date.

"One of the salient features of the modern world", we read at the start of Part I, Chapter 2 [GS 23], "is the growing interdependence of men one on the other", and throughout the Constitution this theme recurs. "Every day human interdependence grows more tightly drawn and spreads by degrees over the whole world" [GS 26]. "[The] human family is gradually recognising that it comprises a single world community and is making itself so" [GS 33]. "Little by little a more universal form of human culture is developing ... the world is becoming unified" [GS 54-5]. "The whole human family ... [is] moving gradually together and everywhere more conscious already of its onenes" [GS 77]. Thirty years before the term achieved any kind of general currency, the Second Vatican Council identified globalisation - economic, political, cultural, and moral - as one of the defining features of modernity. *Gaudium et spes* is not dated - if anything it is a tract more for our times than for the times in which it was written. The most significant cultural development since 1965, the explosion of information and communications technology, above all of the internet, only bears out what it says about our growing knowledge of our interdependence. In fact, one of the most perceptive commentators on the American cultural scene has identified Teilhard de Chardin, whose subterranean influence on this particular Council document was not always appreciated at the time, as one of the conceptual originators of the internet. *Gaudium et spes* gives an account of the modern world which is recognisably contemporary - in §61 it even notes the role of sport in establishing a global culture - and it tells us where in that modern world the Church should be, and where to a great extent it already is. For the world, it says, is changing, and that change is making the world more, not less, accessible to the good news the Church has to preach. We are "witnesses of the birth of a new humanism, one in which man is defined first of all by his responsibility toward his brothers and toward history" [GS 55]. And it is the Church that understands most fully what that definition implies, and what therefore it means to be human. For the Church can see in that responsibility to fraternity and history a responsibility to God, and to God's plan that "by the subjection of all things to man the name of God would be wonderful in all the earth" [GS 34]. Without that insight into the intrinsic human orientation towards God, the new humanism will be unable to understand its object, for "when God is forgotten the creature itself grows unintelligible" [GS 36]. However, what is new about the humanism of what is called the modern world is precisely its potentially theological dimension, its openness to some of the oldest strands in Christian thought. Far from moving away into secular opposition to Christianity, the new humanism is drawing closer to the sacred heart of Christianity, its reconciliation of the secular and the religious, of Man and God.

The crucial step - the crux - that makes it possible for the self-understanding of the modern world to overcome a perhaps five hundred year-old alienation from Christianity is, the Council tells us in its Introductory

Statement, that "the human race has passed from a rather static concept of reality to a more dynamic, evolutionary one" [GS 5]. The purpose of *Gaudium et spes* is to demonstrate how far this new evolutionism is consonant with the far older and fundamental evolutionism of Christianity. The dynamism, intellectual, technological, economic, and ultimately political, that is characteristic of modern society is to be shown to conform to a Christian concept rooted in the New Testament and in the mission of Christ Himself - the concept of 'God's plan'.

> "The divine plan is that man should subdue the earth, bring creation to perfection, and develop himself. When a man so acts he simultaneously obeys the great Christian commandment that he place himself at the service of his brother men" [GS 57].

Strictly speaking, then, it is not the dynamism, the striving of the human family to "accomplish its task of constructing for all men everywhere a world more genuinely human" [GS 77], that is characteristic of modernity, but the awareness of it - not the evolution, for that has been going on all the time, but the evolutionism. In recent centuries, the evolution has become so rapid that society has been forced to become aware of it and - largely as a result of historical accident - it has often expressed that awareness in terms independent of the Christian terms in which alone it can make ultimate sense. In *Gaudium et spes*, the Council set itself the task of demonstrating both what is compatible with Christianity, and even implicitly Christian, about the language developed by the modern world for describing social change, and what must be added to it to make it fully and explicitly Christian.

So let us now consider, first, the anthropological account given in *Gaudium et spes* of the human vocation, and then the modifications to it that are said to be necessary if it is to become an explicitly Christian account.

The systematic element in the structure of *Gaudium et spes* is particularly apparent in the Second Part, despite the understated title and subtitles which suggest we are dealing only with 'some problems' or 'some principles', as if they were a fairly arbitrary selection of topics, offered in no particular order. Yet the sequence of themes is at once recognisable as in outline that of the great anthropologies of the idealist Enlightenment, for example, the third section of Hegel's *Philosophy of Right*. Like the Council, and like Thomas Aquinas, but unlike most of his own French and British predecessors, Hegel believes that Man is intrinsically a social being, and therefore he holds, again like the Council, that an account of concrete social existence must begin, not with a notional pre-social individual, but with marriage and the family. He then proceeds - as, after a detour, which I shall discuss shortly, does *Gaudium et spes* - to the economic community and civil society; after that to the political community, or state, which resolves various contradictions internal to civil society, in which context he treats, as does the Council, of the relations between Church and State; and finally, and again like the Council, he deals with relations between states, with issues of peace and war, and with questions about the shape of world-history. I draw attention to this parallel, which is not necessarily particularly remarkable in itself, in order to point up how comprehensive is the systematic ambition concealed beneath those modest subtitles, and also for the sake of the revealing points of difference, the points where *Gaudium et spes* is manifestly not Hegelian, despite its closeness to idealism and its encyclopaedic scope.

What the Constitution does have in common with Hegelianism, one of the earliest forms of the modern world's secular evolutionism, is the belief that a drive towards universality can be found in all forms of social interaction, even the most specific. The goal of "a universal brotherhood" [GS 38] is written into the most fundamental processes of society. The labour of men and women to meet the immediate needs of themselves and their families, is, we are told in GS 34, already a contribution to society and so ultimately to the realisation in history of God's mysterious purpose. Work, and the results of work, do not merely procure the passing satisfaction of the desire to consume, but through doing so they increase the area of social interaction and so increase the area of morally meaningful behaviour: "For the greater man's power becomes, the farther his individual and community responsibility extends" [GS 34]. The fundamental purpose of the great growth in economic productivity, which is so characteristic of the modern world, must be the benefit "of every man whatsoever and every group of men, of whatever race and from whatever part of the world" [GS 64]. Indeed the potential scope of the justice and charity [GS 69] which economic collaboration makes it possible to exercise extends, according to GS 70, not just to those currently alive but to the people of the future. It is because economic relationships on their own are not adequate to the demands of universal brotherhood, even when those demands are not given a Christian expression, that political institutions arise, so that these too have an innate orientation towards a universal purpose:

> "Individuals, families, and various groups which compose the civic community are aware of their own insufficiency in the matter of establishing a fully human condition of life. They see the need for that wider community in which each would daily contribute his energies toward the ever better attainment of the common good. It is for this reason that they set up the political community ..." [GS 74].

But beyond the common good of the political community or nation lies, GS84 tells us, the "universal common good". The "increasingly close" "bonds of mutual dependence ... between all citizens and all the peoples of the world" impose "modern obligations" which can be met only by the establishment of 'international agencies' and "some universal public authority acknowledged as such by all, and endowed with effective power to safeguard, on the behalf of all, security, regard for justice, and respect for rights" [GS 82]. Dated? These are the burning issues of our time.

In order to address them, however, the Council has at this point to part company with Hegel, who refused to allow the onward drive of his thinking towards universality to project him into speculation about the future, and who saw no right as higher than the might of the individual state, and has to turn instead to Hegel's predecessor Kant, whose treatise *On Perpetual Peace* is alluded to in GS 82. If the meaningfulness of moral choices in the present is to be preserved, Kant believes that such choices must be directed towards the achievement of an ideal state of affairs in the future; if they are not, then at the political level the only alternative to perpetual peace secured by international agreement is the perpetual peace of the graveyard. As *Gaudium et spes* puts it, "it is our clear duty ... to strain every muscle as we work for the time when all war can be completely outlawed by international consent", for if we do not "humanity will perhaps be brought to that mournful hour in which it will experience no peace other than the dreadful peace of death" [GS 82].

Unlike Hegel, then, the Council does not see the dynamic innate to social structures as culminating in any present political institution, such as a state - it is that view of Hegel's, not any doctrine of the Council's, that deserves to be called dated. Instead the Council sees the goal of that dynamic as a kingdom that it is most earnestly incumbent on us to work for, even though - or rather, because - as Christians we know that it can only be achieved by God's grace (if we could not count on God's grace we would have to despair). But this reassessment of the goal of history has an interesting consequence which further differentiates the Council's account of social evolution from that of Hegel. For in Hegel's scheme the space, as we may call it, beyond the individual states, and their rise and fall in world history, is occupied not by any imperative to establish an international order, not by anything moral at all: it is occupied by the realm of absolute knowledge represented by art, religion, and philosophy. In *Gaudium et spes*, art and philosophy, in the broadest sense - religion is obviously a rather different matter - belong under the heading of 'culture' and are treated in a chapter which lies between the chapter on the family and the chapter on the socio-economic, or 'civic', community.   Culture is therefore presented as the first form of the wider world, the world of the wider responsibility for the common good, to which children are introduced by their families [GS 61], before they venture out as economic agents themselves into what Hegel calls 'civil society'.   This transition, from the family to civil society, is called by Hegel a confrontation with 'the particular', that is, with a particular, historically and ethnically specific form of social life - one leaves the world of the family, which in a sense is the same everywhere, and becomes a member of a specific tribe or nation. And that essentially is how the Council presents 'culture', in all its aspects: as something particular, born of national, that is, historically and geographically determined, traditions, aspiring no doubt to universality, but not universal by its nature. While the Council, naturally, sees the religious perspective as comprehending all others, even that of world history, art and philosophy are separated from it and understood as part of the historical and social process.

This point should make us reflect for a moment on the course taken by the theology of culture over the last forty years. For in that period we have seen the rise and rise of the aesthetic theology, or theological aesthetic, of the Germanist turned theologian Hans Urs von Balthasar, not known for his sympathetic attitude either to *Gaudium et spes* or to much of the work of the Council. It is one of the manifest weaknesses of Balthasar's writing - I speak as a Germanist and literary critic, not as a theologian - that he uses concepts of art, beauty and the aesthetic, derived from the German Idealist tradition, which detach the cultural products of quite different traditions from their social and historical context and associate them instead directly with religious revelation. This has the effect, not only of limiting or even falsifying the interpretation of the products he chooses to deal with, but also of excluding from his consideration entire areas of culture, particularly mass culture, such as the realistic novel or the film, which have profound anthropological, moral, and so religious significance, but which for one reason or another are looked down on by the Idealist aesthetic. More seriously still, when we come to consider the questions of international order and the future of humanity raised in the final chapters of *Gaudium et spes*, Balthasar's maintenance of the Hegelian association of art, philosophy, and religion, from which the Council so clearly wished to distance itself, restores also the Hegelian priority of absolute knowledge over moral imperatives. Kant is driven out, the future is closed off, and it becomes more important to see ourselves as walk-on actors in an eschatological artwork than to strain every muscle to extend the kingdom of justice, love, and peace. If *Gaudium et spes* is a document of unparalleled courage, Balthasar is a theologian for a Church that has lost its nerve.

Courage is not to be equated with imprudence. The Council's willing exposition of the immanent purposiveness of human development - of our natural vocation - is not purchased at the price of silence, deliberate or unthinking, about the gospel, the good news of God's grace. I see three main themes in *Gaudium et spes* which link its anthropological vision of our vocation to its theological vision.

First, there is the theme of bodiliness. It is repeatedly stressed that the social processes that are described take place in and through the lives of individual persons, and that a moral, and *a fortiori* a religious, judgement on them cannot abstract from their effect on those individual lives. Because the Church is "at once a sign and a safeguard of the transcendence of the human person" [GS 76], it can never take the statistical or quantitative view of development, which might see a certain amount of disturbance or destruction as acceptable, given its long-term creative advantages. The human person transcends the entire socio-economic, political, and international evolution which is all that a purely anthropological view can see. The human person is the point at which the anthropological evolutionism of *Gaudium et spes* gives way to the theological. For with every human person the essential religious question arises in a way unique to that individual, the question that is so wonderfully posed in the *Declaration on the Relationship of the Church to Non-Christian Religions*: "What ... is that ultimate and unutterable mystery which engulfs our being, and whence we take our rise, and whither our journey leads us?" (*Nostra aetate* 1). But what makes a human person individual, and so able to pose the religious question in their own absolutely unique way? Their body. The emphasis on respect for the body, and on the family life in which bodies are directly produced and nurtured by other bodies, is an essential part of the demonstration in *Gaudium et spes* that the Church is the safeguard of the human person and so that the anthropological perspective needs to be completed by the theological. But it is also one of the peculiarly prophetic aspects of the Constitution, if we consider cultural developments since 1965. I am not referring simply to the continuing instrumentalisation of sexuality that we have seen especially in the Western world, and the illusion which it fosters that bodies, whether our own or other people's, are consumer goods, rather than just us - the medium of our existence, and of our unique question to the mystery. I am thinking also of the concealment of our bodiliness that is a concomitant of the communications revolution which in other respects so obviously manifests our interdependence. The virtual reality of the computer screen fills many lives almost completely, and it has come out on to the streets thanks to the mobile phone: the pedestrians who pass you busily conversing with the ether are now only in an accidental sense bodily close to you, and only an accident is likely to remind the people who gather round it that they are all bodies together in the same place at the same time. These new moral and conceptual demands no more compromise the undoubtedly beneficent, charity-and-fraternity-building character of our ever more wired-up and wire-less society than the commercial exploitation of sex compromises the twentieth-century liberation from much sexual hypocrisy, misery, and cruelty, for which the Church should give thanks more often than it does. But these new demands *are* an opportunity for evangelisation, an opportunity for the Church to show to the world that the comfortable and seemingly self-evident processes of our society are transcended by a mystery present in the most everyday features of our lives.

A second theme also links *Gaudium et spes* with the declaration *On Non-Christian Religions*, where it performs a similar function of opening up to God an anthropological vision of the cultural facts of life in the modern world. It is the principle that certain things are known not to the angels in heaven, nor even to the Son, but only to the

Father. We can see that "the more unified the world becomes, the more plainly do the offices of men extend beyond particular groups and spread by degrees to the whole world", that as a result "individual men and their associations [must] cultivate in themselves the moral and social virtues" and that they may thus become "artisans of a new humanity" [GS 30]. But "we do not know the time for the consummation of the earth and of humanity. Nor do we know how all things will be transformed" [GS 39]. Similarly, in its relations with other religions, the Church must "acknowledge, preserve, and promote the spiritual and moral goods found among [the followers of other religions]" but must await "that day, known to God alone, on which all peoples will address the Lord in a single voice" [NA 2, 4]. It is of faith that Christ died for all men, *Gaudium et spes* tells us at §22, that the "ultimate vocation of man is one", and that "the Holy Spirit ... offers to every man the possibility of being associated with this paschal mystery", but it is equally of faith that the manner in which this offer is made is "known only to God". We cannot spell out, either in the terms used by human wisdom, or even in the terms used by divine wisdom when it speaks with a human voice in the Church, what is Christian in the lives and beliefs of those who do not bear the name of Christ (that surely is the true meaning of the much-abused concept of 'anonymous Christianity' - the Christianity that Christians, not non-Christians, cannot identify). Equally, we cannot spell out what features of the new humanity being built by the secular processes of socialisation will be found again in the eternal and universal kingdom [GS 39], though it is of faith that "the triumphs of the human race are a sign of God's greatness and the flowering of His own mysterious design" [GS 34]. (They are, so to speak, anonymous eschatology.) *Gaudium et spes* has been accused of encouraging Pelagianism, but its great strength is that by insisting on what we do not and cannot know it finds not the fulness but the *signs* of God's greatness among the signs of the times, and so it neither identifies earthly progress with the kingdom of heaven, nor withdraws the Church from the field of purposive human endeavour, as if we knew all the answers already and all we had to do was to keep the rules. We are to live in the world amid the signs of God, restless, like St Augustine, who is alluded to as a model both in *Gaudium et spes* and in *Nostra aetate*, and like him knowing that only in God can we rest.

The third theme in *Gaudium et spes* that structures the relationship between the anthropological and the theological is therefore that of the divine plan itself. Christ is of course the beginning, middle, and end of that plan, and in the concluding section of the Constitution we find its pithiest summary: "the Father wills that in all men we recognise Christ our brother and love Him effectively in word and in deed" [GS 93]. The work of self-perfection, which the anthropologist can discern in the human process of socialisation, is already the fulfilment of a divine intention. "Christians should rejoice that they can follow the example of Christ, who worked as an artisan" [GS 43] because "whoever follows after Christ, the perfect man, becomes himself more of a man" [GS 41]. However the imitation of Christ involves more than the unfolding of the happy consequences of human work, and there is more to the divine work than the anthropologist can see. For the human race has from the beginning failed to do the Father's will, a "spirit of vanity and malice ... transforms into an instrument of sin those human energies intended for the service of God and man", and the "struggle against the powers of darkness ... will continue until the last day" [GS 37]. But by faith we know that Christ "slew hatred in his own flesh", "restoring the unity of all men in one people and one body" [GS 78]. So following his example means that "we too must shoulder that cross which the world and the flesh inflict upon those who search after peace and justice" [GS 38]. Devoting ourselves to realising the divine plan does not mean simply celebrating the triumphs of the human race, though we should be more willing to do that than we have become since 1965: the peaceful end of the Soviet Empire, the eradication of smallpox, the reduction by a third in the number of those in extreme poverty in the single decade of the 1990s, are achievements that deserve celebration. But we must also be prepared to recognise the continuing existence of what the Constitution calls "infamies" - states of affairs in the world that cannot be part of God's plan and that it is therefore incumbent on us to remedy: systems of land tenure, for example, which reduce tenants to a state "unworthy of human beings" [GS 71], or "totalitarian or dictatorial forms" of government which "harm humanity" [GS 75]. The work to which the Christian can see the human race is called is not that of the gradual construction of a perfect world, but that of the permanent reconstruction of a world threatened and damaged by sin: "the good news of Christ constantly renews the life and culture of fallen man" [GS 58]. The image and instrument of the Christian hope which sustains us in that work is at the same time a memorial of the price God has paid to secure it for us, an image in which the work of human hands on the gifts of God is taken up by God and returned to us as a reason for "living and hoping" [GS 31]: "The Lord left behind a pledge of this hope and strength for life's journey in that sacrament of faith where natural elements refined by man are changed into His glorious Body and Blood, providing a meal of brotherly solidarity and a foretaste of the heavenly banquet" [GS 38].

Bishops we are told in §43 of *Gaudium et spes*, "should ... so preach the message of Christ that all the earthly activities of the faithful will be bathed in the light of the gospel". In the last part of what I have to say let me offer some tips for those sermons. Specifically, I should like to narrow down the very general question in my title to a question of some topical interest: where is the Church in modern Europe? What has the Church to say to a European Union in something of an identity crisis? So let us start with the question what is Europe?

I do not think it is helpful to appeal to geographical, historical, or cultural considerations in order to explain what the European Union is, what it is trying to do, and why that is valuable - as was essayed by the drafters of the preamble to the now moribund European Constitution. Those are all considerations that explain why it is easy and natural for certain countries to come together, but not what they come together for - what the purpose of the Union is. Moreover, to give weight to such factors is to risk appearing to exclude or marginalise, a priori, countries that are geographically remote, or culturally different, or whose history offers few links with most of Europe. If you identify Europe by reference to its past, then it is an absurdity not to refer to its Christian roots, but it is not by its past that Europe should seek to be identified. Just as Gaudium et spes identifies the role of the Church in the modern world by reference to humanity's future, so Europe has to look ahead not behind, for it is ahead of us, not behind us, that there lie the reasons for living and hoping. And the Church has to ask itself how it stands, first of all, to Europe's hopes.

Therefore I think the Union should be defined by its threefold commitment: (1) to economic freedom, especially the free movement within the Union of goods, services, capital and labour; (2) to political freedom, specifically the right of all citizens in the Union to take part by means of the vote in all political processes that affect or purport to represent them; and (3) to supranational institutions as the means of ensuring the continuing development of the economic union and of humanising economic processes in accordance with general principles of solidarity. The third point is, I believe, the vital distinguishing feature of the Union. It is the ceding of political power to authorities which transcend the nation that makes the EU unique on the planet, and a sign - a prophetic sign - for the future of humanity. No other international bodies approach the institutions of the EU in the degree to which, by a consensus always ultimately derived from the authority of the vote, they can regulate what in the past were regarded as internal affairs of a nation, nor is there any parallel for the degree of integrated co-operation achieved by the EU in economic and to some extent legal affairs (even if in other respects integration is not so pronounced).

The Church must surely endorse these fundamental principles of the Union as conducive to the peace, prosperity, and mutual support of the Union's members, for one lesson we can certainly draw from *Gaudium et spes* is that the Church is properly concerned to see the elimination, or at least reduction, of the evils of war, poverty, and selfishness. Our Lord came that we might have life and have it more abundantly, and the Church should rejoice in anything that so clearly and substantially fosters human flourishing - not least because there are not many voices in Europe to express such a message. In an atmosphere of Euroscepticism or resigned Euro-apathy, of narrow-minded concern with what is thought of as national advantage, or neurotic fear of what is thought of as the loss of national sovereignty or identity, it is already a prophetic act to point to what is morally and theologically good about the material and social progress made possible by the Union.

In other words, the Church - not even as Catholic, but simply as Christian - can give to the Union a moral and religious value that will not be visible to those who see it as an alien structure with which their own sectional interest makes a series of compromises for the sake of what they hope will be a net positive balance. The Church can welcome the development of the Union as a whole, and can encourage all the members of the Union to rise above their local concerns and share in a perspective in which all progress of the Union, and especially its extension, is a reason to be glad. The Union is a good thing for all European people - the Church can say that, and can give reasons for saying that, as no national government can say it, and as not even the European institutions themselves can say it (for a national government would sound hypocritical, and the institutions would sound self-satisfied). The Union is doing what is right and what God wants for the people of Europe, for God wants them to live in peace, contentment, and mutual love, has implanted the desire for such a life in human nature, and has expressed its rightness in the natural law.

The fundamental evolutionism of *Gaudium et spes* also corresponds to the intrinsically dynamic nature of the European identity that the Union defines. Whenever Europe opens itself further to the world system and transcends its former boundaries - as when it accepts new members - it reinforces its identity; and whenever it seeks to retreat into itself and construct a European fortress - as when it seeks to make itself into a defensive regional bloc - it sins against its own spirit. Its spirit is that not of the melting pot but of the ever-closer union, not of *e pluribus unum* but of what we might call collegiality,

The old Europe, the Europe that very largely coincided with what was called Christendom, had definite geographical and cultural boundaries. It stopped clearly at the Atlantic and the Hellespont, somewhat less clearly somewhere east of Kiev, and it certainly did not include the Islamic world, except provisionally as the invading or occupying Turk or Moor. The political structure of the new Europe already all but fills out the boundaries of the old, and already we know that in concept and in principle it transcends them. It is thinkable that one day Russia could be an applicant for membership of the Union and to think that thought is to recognise that at a stroke Europe could acquire a Pacific coastline. More immediate, and more fundamental, is the prospect raised by the application of Europe's long-standing adversary Turkey, the accession of which would seem finally to destroy any link between Europe and old Christendom. But it would be an enlargement of Europe entirely in accordance with the spirit of variety and collegiality and so of old Christendom too. For medieval Christendom is unthinkable without Islam. Both were inheritors, not only of Judaism and the conflicts that divided early Christianity, but of the culture and political structures of the Roman Empire. It is a commonplace that without the return to Western Europe of the Greek philosophy that Islam had kept alive, we should not have the defining conceptual structure of medieval and modern Christianity, the theology of Thomas Aquinas. Islam was for Christendom the Other that it knew, not the Other (like say pre-Columban America) of which it knew nothing. So the accession of an Islamic nation to the European Union would restore the cultural perspectives of Christendom and perhaps begin the task of reconciling contradictions to which the medieval world proved unequal. And if Turkey, why not, one day, Israel (already a contributor to the Eurovision Song Contest)? The process of economic and political pacification and co-ordination that is Europe's ever-closer union has no clear or necessary territorial or cultural bounds. It will stop only when the supply of applicants dries up. It can be envisaged as a multi-faith, multi-cultural, multi-speed and multi-level union of former nations, bound together by their commitment to the free market, democracy, and the rule of supranational institutions. As the Christian Church comes to understand better its relation to other faiths, so it will find it easier to see in such a Union a clear contribution to the natural fulfilment of a divine plan.

But of course the Christian Church also knows - it is its distinctive message - that human goodness is achievable not as a simple fulfilment of our nature - a simple culmination of our natural desires - but only as a triumph over sin. There is no goodness in the world that is not marked by the sacrificial death of God in Christ for our sake - no goodness that is not a recovery (by God) of a goodness that we had lost. There is no goodness that is not sin forgiven. And so Europe's history, its geographical and cultural specificity, is relevant after all. For whatever good the EU has brought, and promises for the future, is the sunlit summit of a mountain of sin. If we rejoice in the flourishing, of which it is both the gift and the sign, we must also recognise the sin out of which it has come and which only God can forgive. The territorial and religious wars, the expulsions and persecutions, in which the modern European nations had their origin, the monstrous destruction of human life and happiness in the urban hells and devastated countryside of the era of Industrial Revolution, the cruelty and contempt with which the Imperial nations enslaved and made tributary the non-European world in the name of global commerce, the World Wars and genocide that, originating in twentieth-century Europe, marked the collapse of those Imperial ventures, all the personal and collective wickedness that went to make the Europe of today - those are the dark clouds of the Flood which have made it possible for such signs of God's forgiveness as the establishment of the state of Israel, or the new hope embodied in the European Union, to shine out like the rainbow of the Covenant. These signs of the times can be read only by the Church of the crucified and risen Christ.

But the voice of the Church must be not only prophetic but also messianic. The task of the prophet is not only to read the past, so as to understand the present, but to look to the future in anticipation and warning. The undeniable (but often denied) human good that the EU brings is a good that comes marked not only by the sin of whose forgiveness it is a sign, but by the sin of which it may yet prove the occasion. Our Lord forgave the adulterous woman but warned her to sin no more, and his injunction to Peter to be prepared after forgiving his brother once to forgive him another seventy times seven was, whatever else it may have been, a realistic assessment of human weakness. Like the establishment of the state of Israel, the establishment and growth of the EU is a great sign to the world of the possible triumph of hope and peace and the goodness of God over fear and war and human evil. But as the prophets repeatedly warn, it is open to humanity to waste and spoil God's gift and make it the source, perhaps, of even greater evil than it was its purpose to heal. The gift of God is a test, too, and the messianic kingdom is a time of judgement as well as of fulfilment. The question of Israel's temptation, however topical, is not a question we need address here, but a warning surely needs to be uttered about the temptations consequent on the enlargement of the EU which the euphoria of 2004 may conceal. The temptation I think is twofold: it has an internal and an external aspect. Internally, there is the risk of accelerating the processes of consumption and favouring the interests of the consumer, while forgetting that we are all producers too, for whom work itself is a value, and who have, as workers, interests to be protected, especially in the work that we do in reproducing ourselves through family life. A larger and more effective Union could become a soulless mechanism remote from the atomised individuals who make it up and who might lose all collective local and personal identity, being reduced to mere economic units that are a prey to anomie and alienation and seek to drown their despair in ever more frantic consumption. Externally, there is a converse risk, far more serious, for it affects many more people. It is the risk that the Union will consider only its own interests as a producer bloc and seek to build itself an economic fortress behind high tariff walls and immigration quotas instead of heeding the sign it is itself giving to the world. That is the sign of ever-growing economic interaction under the control of supranational institutions. It is the nature of the Union, the source of its identity, that it should seek to surpass itself, enlarge itself beyond any particular set of boundaries and extend its threefold commitment until it can apply to the whole world. The Union would contradict itself, the purpose for which it exists, if it were to try to become a super-nation, asserting its own interests as an ultimate value for all its members, and ignoring the extent to which the economic processes it sets out to foster involve and affect large numbers of people all over the planet.

The Common Agricultural Policy in particular is a serious temptation to sin for the enlarged Union - a temptation to sacrifice the interests of the very poor in the developing world to the interests of the less poor in its unmodernised agricultural sectors. The ambition to establish a Union defence capacity is also potentially an occasion for delusion as to the true nature of the union and so possibly for sin. While pointing to the hope for world peace that the Union represents, when properly understood, the Church, that is those who preach and teach and speak in its name, would do well also to remind the citizens of the Union of the responsibilities of being a messianic sign, which are not compatible with an ambition to strut on the world stage as a hard man with hard elbows.

Specifically as Catholic, the Church is singularly, perhaps uniquely, well placed to deliver the prophetic warning. The world-wide Catholic Church is one of humanity's truly global institutions. Thanks to its collegial structure, the Church whether directly, through its bishops, or indirectly, through its institutions of education, can be the voice in Europe of those who produce and consume outside the borders of the union but whose livelihoods, and very lives, may be determined by what is done and decided within them. Ultimately the destiny of the Union is to give a controlling and humanising political structure to those extended economic relationships too. The European Church - urged on no doubt by its fellows in the global communion - can help to keep that destiny in the minds of Europe's citizens when they are tempted to forget that they owe their prosperity to their willingness to accept supranational, and so eventually even supra-continental, restraint.

The Church can be Europe's global conscience when it is tempted into regional narrow-mindedness. But the Catholic Church is not only the universal church - it is also the local church which brings God's sacramental presence into particular places, particular communities and particular lives. It can therefore be Europe's local conscience too, warning the Union when it is failing in its duty of justice and care towards the identities - nations or cultures or individuals in localities - that have subordinated themselves to the Union as the greater good and as the guardian of equity. The Church can speak, whether at the level of local communities, or of nations or of the Union itself, for those who are not part of the cycle of production and consumption - for those who cannot work, whether through disability or unemployment, for those whose work, in bearing and bringing up children for example, is not rewarded with the power to consume - and for those aspects of creation, human, animal, vegetable, or mineral, that are not agents in the process of production and consumption though they may be profoundly affected by it or even be its material: the life of human feeling, for example, that is refined or degraded by the media; the animals and plants that we feed on or exploit; the biosphere and the landscape that we alter, functionalise or pollute. Through the sacraments of the Church God comes as Saviour into this world of physical immediacy and spiritual and emotional individuality, just as through the sacraments, that is through the Church, as a whole, God is present to the global system. As those who both dispense the sacraments locally, and build up the Church, universally, the bishops of the Catholic Church can judge, and say aloud, how far the Union is staying true to its mission, which in the long term is a mission to the whole of the modern world.

GAUDIUM ET SPES: THE UNADDRESSED ISSUES

Archbishop Diarmuid Martin argues that the great contribution of *Gaudium et spes* to the life of the church was its commitment to evaluating the signs of the times in the light of the Gospel. Contrary to some opinion, this involved an appraisal of *both* the hopes and joys *and* the sorrows and anxieties of the mid-twentieth century. Today, fidelity to the process set in motion forty years ago requires that whole church stay alert to the gifts and griefs of the twenty-first century. He argues in particular for a new generation of articulate lay Christians who are prepared to take the dialogue initiated at Vatican II into a new and changing world.

If you take any collection of the conciliar texts of Vatican II, like that of Austin Flannery, you will find in addition to the texts of the Constitutions and Decrees themselves also a collection of subsequent documents issued by the Holy See regarding the implementation of those documents. That is not the case for *Gaudium et spes*. There are no tailor-made guidelines for its application. The programme of the Pastoral Constitution emerges more as a process than as a doctrine.

It is clear that the nature and the originality of the Pastoral Constitution meant that it would have to be implemented in a very different way to the other Council documents. Some would even say that perhaps the term implementation cannot be applied to *Gaudium et spes*. Others would go as far as to say that the shelf life of such a document was by its nature short, tentative or limited and *Gaudium et spes* would have to be, if not rewritten, then at least 're-mediated' into the different social and economic situation which emerged as the years went by. Others still would say that through its own affirmation of "the rightful autonomy of earthly things" the further interpretation of the Pastoral Constitution would be determined by developments in the social and economic sciences rather than principally by theological or pastoral interpretations.

Gaudium et spes was, in fact, the object of an interpretative document and has been revisited in the years after the Council. The Special Session of the Synod of Bishops in 1985, for example, dedicated a great deal of its time to the way in which *Gaudium et spes* had been interpreted over the years, and despite a feeling of anxiety at the time that a programme of going back on the Council was underway, that Synod reaffirmed the Pastoral Constitution and its value. Many will remember that an interview with Cardinal Ratzinger speaking of "restoration" was interpreted in terms of rejecting the Council, something which in fact was never the case. The final document of that Special Session of the Synod noted with clarity:

> "The Church as communion is a sacrament for the salvation of the world... In this context we affirm the great importance and timeliness of the Pastoral Constitution *Gaudium et spes*".[45]

The document then adds:

> "At the same time, however, we perceive that the signs of our time are in part different from the time of the Council, with greater problems and anguish. Today, in fact, everywhere in the world we witness an increase in hunger, oppression, injustice and war, sufferings, terrorism and other forms of violence of every sort. This requires a new and

---

[45]   Synod of Bishops, "The Final Report" in *Origins NC Documentary Service*, 1985, December 19th, Vol. 15, No. 27, pp . 444-450: 449

more profound theological reflection in order to interpret these signs in the light of the Gospel".[46]

One can see here again the understanding of *Gaudium et spes* as an ongoing process of dialogue between the Gospel message and the signs of the times in which new and previously unaddressed issues would be taken up.

The verification of the application of *Gaudium et spes* and of what form of *aggiornamento* it has brought to the Church is more difficult, then, than with other documents. It can only be done within the context of developments in both Church and contemporary society and of their interaction. The process of evaluation is such also that it takes place in a situation in which the pace of social change has been way beyond anything that the authors of the document could have foreseen. The Pastoral Constitution did indeed recognise that change was taking place and that this change was epoch making. It notes that "humanity is passing through a new phase in its history in which profound and rapid changes are gradually affecting the whole world" [GS 4]. I am not sure, however, that bishops of Vatican II really recognised how the pace of such change would accelerate in the years subsequent to the Council.

Gaudium et spes speaks about the "upheavals" which society at the time had to address [GS 5]. It noted that society was moving from a "static to a dynamic and evolutionary conception of things" [GS 5]. But it still looked at the development of an industrial society and was unable even to imagine what a post-industrial world would look like and the effects that an information revolution and a knowledge-based economy would have.

---

[46]   Synod of Bishops, "The Final Report": 449

If the document underestimated the pace of change in the society, it probably underestimated even more the changes that would take place in the Church.

The world and the Church of today have changed so much since the 1960s. *Gaudium et spes* predates 1968! And by 1968 I think both of the student revolt and of the publication of *Humanae vitae*. It predates the fall of the Central and Eastern European communist regimes. It predates the era of globalisation. No government or organisation would today present as its flagship formula for the interpretation of its place in society, as its "mission statement", something written forty years ago! In that sense, we would have to look at the entire contemporary social, political and economic horizon, with all its radical change, as an unaddressed issue of *Gaudium et spes.*

The most important change in contemporary society since the publication of *Gaudium et spes,* and the one which requires most attention, regards anthropology, the vision of the human person that is the driving force of contemporary reflection. Pope John Paul II from the beginning of his Pontificate saw the centrality of this question as few others have. His first Encyclical, *Redemptor hominis*, was focused on the human person as the way of the Church. He stressed both the theory and the practice of human rights, a theme which was not fully elaborated in *Gaudium et spes*. Throughout his Pontificate he indicated also how difficult and challenging such a dialogue with the anthropological vision of current society, especially Western society, could be.

At the time of the publication of *Gaudium et spes* there was a certain optimism in the air about the possibility of creating a better future. The Council itself and the miracle that Pope John XXXIII seemed to have achieved in ecumenical dialogue contributed to this optimism and it was in tune with this optimism. There has been much discussion about the overall thrust of *Gaudium et spes* regarding the fundamental goodness or frailty of human nature itself. Many would say today that *Gaudium et spes* was over-optimistic about the human project or the capacity of humankind to ensure that the good would prevail. *Gaudium et spes* spoke about dialogue with contemporary culture, but just as Pope John Paul II stressed, that dialogue was one in which the message of Jesus Christ must appear as the unique corner-stone. The Church desires to understand modern culture, but only the redeeming power of Jesus is capable of overcoming the presence of sin and evil in the world.

The Church's much desired dialogue with atheism had to find new ways in the changed geopolitical landscape and address more the atheism of indifference, the practical atheism of many and the atheism of Western culture.

The 1985 Synod addressed this question in terms of the Mystery of the Cross: "It seems to us that in the present-day difficulties God wishes to teach us more deeply the value, the importance and the centrality of the cross of Jesus Christ. Therefore the relationship between human history and salvation is to be explained in the light of the paschal mystery. Certainly the theology of the cross does not at all exclude the theology of the creation and incarnation, but, as is clear, it presupposes it. When we Christians speak of the cross, we do not deserve to be labelled pessimists, but rather found ourselves upon the realism of Christian hope".

Gaudium et spes was however a careful document. For the Council the human condition always remains an "enigma" [GS 18]. The document contains many of the *caveats* that some of its opponents seem to have ignored. The optimism of *Gaudium et spes* is certainly captivating. Its cautionary tones, however, were often played down. I often think of the many bishops who have taken *Gaudium et spes* as their motto but I have yet to meet one who has taken as his motto the second phrase of the opening sentence of the Pastoral Constitution: *Luctus et angor,*: "Sorrow and Anxiety". (I say that, referring at least to a written motto. Many may have taken those words as a programme of life).

It should be noted that *Gaudium et spes* itself is probably more realistic than some of its interpreters or interpretations. In many ways this was due to correctives introduced during the writing of the document, especially by Bishops from the German-speaking lands, who had experienced how human nature and the minds of people could be deviated into the most extraordinary of evil enterprises, such as that of the holocaust. *Gaudium et spes* from its first paragraph onwards draws attention to the ambivalence of human history, "enslaved to sin" and marked by both the "triumphs and disaster" of the enterprise of humankind [GS 2]. It takes up the famous words of the Letter to the Romans: "Man weak and sinful often does what he would prefer not to do and fails to do what he would he like" [GS 10].

Forty years onwards, as we face the future, we have to recapture some of that biblical realism. In those forty years war has continued, we have had the Rwandan genocide; a brutal war in the heart of Europe in the Balkans; we have had continuous wars right across Africa; ever more violent forms of terrorism and hostage-taking have exploded on the world scene; economic, social and sexual exploitation have continued; hunger and malnutrition are still the order of the day. Christians should be in the forefront in the battle against such evils. They must work with all those who share the same concern. But they must be careful to avoid the superficial and the clichéd. Their commitment must be coherent. It must not be limited to the occasional outburst of global solidarity such as that on the occasion of the Tsunami, or the more militant enthusiasm engendered in these days around the G8 meeting. For the Christian, solidarity should be the stuff of everyday. It is not the solidarity of the dramatic protest but a constant and purposeful commitment in society.

Christian comment on and commitment within society must be rooted in a truly Christian understanding of the human person and the reality of human sinfulness and therefore of the redeeming message of Jesus. Today so many people do not feel the need for redemption. Those who live in prosperity, even a prosperity that is hard-earned, tend to become entrapped in their prosperity and in a logic of material prosperity. The anthropology of *Gaudium et spes* is one which demands solidarity as an imperative and not an option, a daily imperative and not an occasional awakening of conscience. The Christian believer must be fully present in the human enterprise, bringing to it the irreplaceable light of Christ.

This does not of course mean that we fall into a sort of Christian fundamentalism in which we feel that our faith gives us a direct answer to every contemporary challenge. The word has to be mediated through human reflection and human science. But neither can the individual Christian - or Church organisation for that matter - be involved in the work of human advancement just alongside others, especially where there is no common anthropology or indeed there is hostility to Christian anthropology. The anthropology of *Gaudium et spes* is a Christological anthropology. I see here one of the real challenges for the future presence of the Christian in a pluralist, yet at times not totally tolerant, society, especially regarding the role of religion. As opposed to the cultural climate at the time of the publication of *Gaudium et spes* there are many who no longer find it necessary to resort to religious principles to foster an ethic of solidarity. Many have become openly hostile to the offer of a Christian contribution. Religious expression, at times, finds a difficult welcome except on the margins of the public square.

A huge challenge in this dialogue around anthropology is the relationship between the individual human person and that of the human family, of human kind. The great temptation today is to read the concept of human person in terms of current-day individualism, with all its ramifications, especially in terms of individual rights, individual attainment, and individual fulfilment. *Gaudium et spes* attempts to show the interrelationship between the individual and his or her responsibilities in and for society. The danger is that the reader today is unconsciously applying different interpretations of those terms than the Council itself would have done.

This challenge is most acute today, forty years after the publication of *Gaudium et spes*, in the area of marriage and the family. The dominant individualistic trends in philosophy and in popular culture go so far as to make it impossible for many today to fully understand the vision of marriage and the family that is to be found in the Council document.

The Church needs urgently to address the question of an anthropology of human sexuality and marriage, the "first form of personal communion" [GS 12]. The teaching of *Gaudium et spes* on marriage as a personal community enriched the lives of many couples. Concepts of sexual and reproductive rights have, however, been defined in many ways in an exclusively individualistic framework, thus making it impossible to incorporate into them the dimension of mutuality which is of the essence of human sexuality. Let me make it clear that the concept of mutual respect between husband and wife does not exclude, rather it puts flesh on, the right to individual respect and non-exploitation which belongs intrinsically to each of the spouses as human beings. Married persons do not relinquish their individual rights.

It would be foolish to pretend that all of our Christians would fully subscribe today to the vision of marriage and the family contained in *Gaudium et spes*. Many young people have acclimatised themselves to the values of contemporary society. Many do not wish to marry formally. Many if not most will live together for shorter or longer periods before they finally get married. Divorce is not desired but most of our Christian believers would consider it not just a necessary evil but perhaps even a valuable institution. It is interesting that many of those young people who set out on such a path develop into excellent spouses and parents, learning marital and parental abilities you might say from nature itself rather than through any formal catechesis on the part of the Church.

I am not sure that we have fully grasped what are the long-term consequences of this pervasive secularisation and individualisation in marriage. We have to find new ways of going against the current and of stressing the value of mutuality in marriage and the value of marriage as an institution, and not just in sacramental terms, but in terms of what it signifies for society. If we simply stand aside and drift along with contemporary culture we will have failed to bring to our societies precisely the type of constructive engagement between the Gospel message and contemporary culture that was called for by *Gaudium et spes*.

It would be hard to deny that there is a certain reluctance on the part of many Catholics to engage in open debates even on central issues concerning marriage and family as a "good" for society. To a certain degree, this may be the result of the post *Humanae vitae* debates on conscience which may have led to a certain "privatisation" of Catholic thinking on marriage and sexuality. It is a question, I believe, we have to address. Marriage and the family are too fundamental to human and Christian anthropology and our teachings must be articulated and defended.

A similar tension between individual initiative and common responsibility applies to the Church's attitude to modern liberal economic theory. The economic realities of our time are very different to those at the time of the publication of *Gaudium et spes*. There has been a move away from a stress on the role of the State to one in which the positive aspects of the market and of human economic initiative are stressed, albeit with due reservations regarding the limits of the market which were well articulated in *Centesimus annus*. Once again anthropological issues are often at the heart of the debate. Pope John Paul II's concept of a right to economic activity is linked with his view of the creativity and subjectivity which is present in the human person which gives rise also to a subjectivity of society. In a knowledge-based society the human person, human initiative and human creativity are the driving force of economic development.

Such a vision of economic development requires a new understanding of investing in human capacity. Poverty is the inability to realise God-given potential. Fighting poverty is above all about investing in people. It is about finding the ways - financial and technical - to ensure that people can realise their talents and improve their capacity. Perhaps the Church had not got it so wrong in the past when most of its development work was in the field of education.

A challenge for the future is to develop a new vision of the preferential option for the poor. This means not just having general programmes for human advancement but ways in which those who are on the margins are brought into the virtual circle of inclusion. This means improving human capacity, but also broadening the appreciation of what it is to be human and moving away from a dominantly economic vision of society into one where a broader understanding of human purpose and hope can prosper. Any form of globalisation which only increases exclusion has no title to call itself global.

The fundamental principle to guide a globalisation of inclusion is the principle of *Gaudium et spes* concerning the universal destiny of the earth's resources. It needs to be developed in terms appropriate to a knowledge-based society. The question of private property needs to be addressed also in terms of intellectual property. The goods of the earth are not just land and capital, but today also knowledge and the fruits of human genius. We still have not been able to place the fruits of science at the service of the human community. It is stunning to note that the cost of providing antiretroviral medicines needed to fights AIDS could fall in four years from a rate of $10,000 a year per person to the current $150, and this simply through a more thorough application of existing exceptions from intellectual property regimes.

Gaudium et spes really never developed any reflections on the integrity of creation and environmental questions. This is made up to some extent now in the *Compendium of the Social Doctrine of the Church* which has brought together much of the biblical and magisterial teaching on this area.[47]

---

[47]   Pontifical Council For Justice And Peace, *Compendium of the Social Doctrine of the Church*, Washington, USCCB Publishing, 2005

One of the most difficult discussions during the drafting of *Gaudium et spes* was on the theme of war. When I arrived as the Holy See's representative in Geneva, I presented my credentials to the then Head of the UN Office there, a wise and wily former Soviet civil servant who has spent most of his time in disarmament work. He was regarded as belonging to the better of the old-school communists, prudent and cautious yet aware of the realities of international insecurity.

I remember well that after a minimum of formalities we got straight into discussions on disarmament. He reminded me that he was personally involved in the negotiations of the principal UN disarmament or arms control documents. And he said: "let us be clear these are all cold-war documents, and they are becoming less and less adequate to the international situation today. But we have a potential disaster scenario before us. There is an inability or unwillingness to work towards new arms-control frameworks and at the same time the edifice of existing documents is beginning to collapse".

There is both truth and wisdom in the insight of the old disarmament practitioner. The Nuclear Non-Proliferation Treaty is still there and hopefully will stand the test of time despite its fragility. Other treaties have been weakened or will never be ratified. During my time in Geneva, just to give one concrete example, right in the midst of the US-driven alarm concerning weapons of mass destruction, especially chemical and biological weapons, we witnessed at the same time how the United States withdrew its support for a protocol on the verification of biological weapons which was in the final stages of a five year negotiation process!

The number of nuclear weapons is fewer, but the number of countries possessing or interested in having nuclear weapons is high. That said, most people killed in wars after the Second World War have been killed with conventional weapons, either high-tech conventional weapons or indeed very low-tech, but reliable and sturdy weapons. Very little progress has been made in introducing sharper control of the movement of conventional weapons and indeed sales of such arms are considered in many cases an important factor in national economic interest.

Church peace movements had perhaps become too linked with the nuclear issue, and as the Soviet-American ideological conflict abated somewhat, and as people felt that a nuclear conflagration was no longer imminent, then the interest in peace questions diminished. It is easy to be against nuclear catastrophe, but to engage with the complex mechanisms of arms production and sales is not so easy. We need a strong peace movement within the Church, not just the witness of the pacifist, but also the mediation of those who can elaborate and evaluate an enlightened ethical framework for arms production.

Pope John Paul took the teaching on the uselessness of war and therefore of the inappropriateness of war as an instrument of resolving international tensions far further than any of his predecessors. He was unafraid to say this to the world and to individual world leaders. It would be important that this anti-war legacy of Pope John Paul be developed in the ever more complex systems of today.

This brings me to the question of the international community, which was treated in the final pages of *Gaudium et spes*. I suppose that I have spent a great deal of my life working in that area which is called the "international community", but I have always affirmed that the international community does not exist, or that it exists only in a very embryonic state. States still make up the real backbone of international relations. International Organisations are made up of member states who act normally on the basis of the primacy of national interest. Even within the most evolved form of international co-operation ever known, namely the European Union, national interest can still be a major driving force for its members. International Conventions are ratified by States. They thus relinquish voluntarily their own sovereignty - but in most cases not definitively.

Global realities and interests exist today more than ever. But we do not have adequate governance structures, to cope with the political and economic interests involved. International norms, like any other system of norms and laws, are there primarily to protect the weak and to curb the arrogance of the powerful.

There has been progress towards the elaboration of certain norms which constitute international law. There are, however, few sanctions available to apply to those who do not respect that law, especially if the non-respect is by powerful nations (and, let me be clear, I am not speaking of the United States alone). In this context, the World Trade Organisation is perhaps one of the most advanced Organisations and has shown that it can tackle large as well as small offenders. The International Criminal court has still to prove itself in reality.

How can the Church renew today the process which *Gaudium et spes* set in action, a renewal in the application of gospel principles to a reading of the signs of the times? One way is the renewing of the social teaching of the Church, and the recent publication of a *Compendium of the Social Doctrine of The Church* is an important sign. But it is important to remember that the social teaching of the Church is not a catalogue of ready-made answers to the problems of our times. Paradoxically, the concept of the social teaching in the

Church seemed to enter into crisis in the years immediately after Vatican II. Many were unhappy with the term doctrine, preferring social teaching or social reflection or social thought. There was the feeling in many places that the social teaching of the Church should be rather a form of social ethic which could be shared by people of various viewpoints, religious or not. There were clashes with different visions of social teaching. The cold war inevitably led to a polarisation of ideologies in social and economic reflection of all types. Certain trends of Liberation theology had assumed a methodology which was flawed by elements of Marxist analysis. In other cases there was confusion between social teaching and outright political manifestos.

The Compendium sets out to offer a theological reading of the signs of the times. It examines the evolution of the revelation of God's love in the history of salvation, especially the revelation of God's Trinitarian love. Each section is introduced by some reflections from scripture, both from the Old and the New Testaments, which stress the religious nature of the social doctrine and the link between social teaching and the mission of the Church. It presents a unified corpus of principles and criteria which draw their origin from the gospels and which are applied to the realities of the times, in order to form Christians to make their own personal responsible judgements on the best manner to stimulate the ideals proposed by the Gospel in contemporary culture. The social doctrine is not however fundamentalist. It requires a form of mediation by the reader, in dialogue with the social sciences, which brings the social thought of the scriptures into dialogue with the dynamics of contemporary social life and culture. At the same time the term "doctrine" draws attention to the fact that the Christian cannot simply decide that anything goes in terms of social conscience and that certain underlying principles of the social doctrine, especially those closest to the kernel of the Church's teaching, have a binding character in their own right.

The Social Doctrine of the Church is above all an instrument to guide the formation of the consciences of Christians, especially Christian lay persons. Even though the Compendium is addressed first of all to Bishops, I would venture to say that the success of the social teaching is not to be measured in the number of Episcopal statements on social issues - many of which of course may indeed be opportune - but in the maturity of the commitment and responsibility by which lay Christians involve themselves in the realisation of a more just and loving society, coherent with Gospel principles.

For me, perhaps the principal challenge we have to face if we want to renew the spirit of *Gaudium et spes* in the Church is that of fostering the specific vocation of lay Christians in the secular sphere. This vocation charges lay men and women to commit themselves to implanting explicitly and less explicitly the values of the Gospel into the realities of the times, using the instrument which *Gaudium et spes* set out as its own, that of *dialogue*. That applies in particular to young Christians, for whom most of the challenges of *Gaudium et spes* are unaddressed issues, at least as regards their own lives. We need a new generation of articulate lay Christians, who are prepared to take the dialogue initiated at Vatican II into a new and changing world, and to engage every aspect of the culture of that world, economic, political and social. We need people who, to use the phrase of Pope Benedict XVI, will allow themselves to be "surprised by the Gospel" and who, following that surprise, bring new hope and meaning into their world.

ECCLESIA CARITATIS:
REASONS FOR LIVING AND HOPING

Cardinal Cormac Murphy O'Connor's closing address to the conference sets out his vision for a Church formed by the Holy Spirit and impelled by the love which is God's self-communication.

Last weekend, I was doing something very much in the spirit of *Gaudium et spes*. The Make Poverty History Rally in Edinburgh on 2 July was organised by a heterogeneous coalition of groups among which, of course, were the Catholic aid agencies, Cafod and Sciaf. I was there with Cardinal Keith O'Brien to lead off the rally, which attracted more than 200,000 people. There were other faith leaders present, as well as celebrities such as Bianca Jagger and the actor Pete Postlethwaite. We were there to raise our voices in advance of the G8 summit. The issue of world poverty, and the measures that need to be taken by our political leaders, are matters of deep importance to us as Christians. They also matter to Bob Geldof and Bono, and to the British Government, as well as to hundreds of thousands of people who applauded the *Live 8* concert.

The Make Poverty History movement is part of a moral awakening, comparable to the movement to abolish slavery, or apartheid. At its heart is a plea for human dignity, a sense that we should be one family at one table, and a protest at the violation of human dignity represented by so many thousand needless deaths across the developing world. By my presence at the Rally, I wanted to show that the Church has seen in this moral awakening a sign of the times which *Gaudium et spes* asks us to look for; and a sign, too, of what the Pastoral Constitution asks us to promote as a Gospel-rooted vision for our fellow

113

human beings, especially those who are vulnerable and are suffering.

Pope Benedict sent to the Rally a message which underlined this. And that he did so by quoting *Gaudium et spes.* His message captures well how the Church should be inserted into the world:

> "The Holy Father… sends greetings to all who are gathered for this event, united by their concern for the welfare of millions of our brothers and sisters afflicted by extreme poverty. As the Second Vatican Council teaches, 'God intended the earth and all it contains for the use of everyone and of all peoples; so that the good things of creation should be available equally to us all' [GS 69]. For this reason, people from the world's richest countries should be prepared to accept the burden of debt reduction for heavily indebted poor countries, and should urge their leaders to fulfil the pledges made to reduce world poverty, especially in Africa, by the year 2015. His Holiness prays for the participants in the rally and for the world leaders soon to gather at Gleneagles, that they may all play their part in ensuring a more just distribution of the world's goods. In the ardent hope that the scourge of global poverty may one day be consigned to history, he cordially imparts his Apostolic Blessing."

If the presence of two cardinals at the head of an anti-poverty coalition, and the Pope's blessing of its aims, raise few eyebrows, that is, of itself, a measure of how the Constitution has transformed us all. Its themes have been taken up and developed in the writings of Paul VI in *Populorum progressio,* and of John Paul II in *Sollicitudo rei socialis,* to name two seminal Encyclicals in a growing corpus.[48] It is not my intention to rehearse these great themes, many of which you will have touched on already. Instead, I want to explore some central but perhaps not so immediate features of *Gaudium et spes*. I do so because I think that forty years on they can still inspire us, continuing to offer us a vision of our mission today and for the future.

Christ invited Peter to "put out into the deep", and at the beginning of our new millennium, Pope John Paul reminded us that this is still Christ's invitation to his Church.[49] The deep is, of course, the inexhaustible mystery of God, and our "putting out" is our absolute confidence in Him. But it is also the inscrutable "deep" of human history, its changes and challenges, which always remain something of an enigma for us. We are asked to "put out into the deep" with confidence, taking the risk of staking everything on Christ and His promise. This is why we set out with real "joy and hope" at his command. It may be that our way is not always clear; we may often worry about the means we have to sustain our mission; it is, after all, a journey of faith. Yet, I believe that the Council has given us both "food for the journey" and orientations so that we are never lost however strange the terrain may be. So, at the end of this conference I want to speak a little about this "food" and some of these "orientations" so that we can continue our journey with confidence.

1. "The Signs of the Times" and the *Kairos* of Faith

I want to consider three aspects that I believe are central to our living as the community of faith in our contemporary world, especially in our own British and European culture. The first concerns the way in which we "discern the signs of the times". The second is the question about how we

---

[48]   Cf. Lab. Ex. 1981 also Cent An. 1991; Etc.
[49]   Novo. Mill. Ine. §1. 6th Jan. 2001

engage the culture we live in, and the third is a short reflection on the sort of Church we are called to be in the world. I want to use these three aspects as ways of gathering up the themes of the conference but also to indicate the richness of the Council's thought that we are still in the process of making our own. Turning to the first: the last forty years have been times of very considerable change internationally and in Britain. They have been times of change for the Church also. I think our task, in all these events, is to "discern the signs of the times." It was the task John XXIII identified when he announced his decision to summon the Council.[50] Indeed, "discerning the signs of the times" is central to the method and intention of *Gaudium et spes*, and it is just as important for us now as it was when the Constitution was written.

The Signs of the Times: Discernment and Freedom

"The signs of the times" is a phrase that trips easily off the tongue and is used in a variety of different contexts. For us, however, it is not primarily about political, historical or cultural analysis; it is about discernment. We do not come to "the times" with the methodological neutrality of the scientist or the professional academic. The Church cannot be neutral regarding humanity or history because we come to it always in the name of Christ, with the knowledge and perspective of the healing gift that the Father has given to the world in his Son through the anointing of the Holy Spirit. God and the destiny that God calls each person to is the horizon within which we read every time. For us, history is a text that we read through the lens of revelation, itself an event within history. This is not an oppressive pre-condition or prejudice; it is not a covert commitment to an ideology or political programme[51]; rather, it is a constant process of

---

[50]   CF. also M-D Chenu, 'The Signs of the Times', in *The Church Today* ed. Group 2000, New York, Newham Press. 1968 pp.43-59.
[51]   Sol. Rei. Soc. § 41.

discerning and judging what best serves the common good and the flourishing of human life and freedom in the light of who Christ reveals us to be. This act of discernment is our commitment, not just to "our" times but also to all future times and generations.

Discernment entails a certain practical realism about what is possible within any given situation. To engage in the Make Poverty History rally requires us to understand why trade, aid and debt can make a difference to world poverty; or how, for example, agricultural subsidies prevent poor countries trading out of poverty. But discernment is not primarily about pragmatic strategies nor is it about realising our own will. Discernment is the search within all the complex and changing circumstances of our lives for God's will. It requires of us a genuine openness and trust, attentiveness to the God who is active in all the movements and obscurities of our historical existence. We know, too, from the rich spiritual and moral tradition of our Church that the first prerequisite of discernment is freedom.

"Freedom" is one of the key words in our society and it can be read in many different ways. I think it is one of the most difficult and misunderstood points of engagement that we have with our culture. You could devote a whole conference to the theme of "freedom", and obviously, this is not the time to undertake a detailed discussion. But it is central to the nature of the Church and the task of discernment and it is important to sketch some elements of our understanding in that context.[52]

The Truth of Christ sets us free, but this is not quite the same as "freedom of choice" or "autonomy", concepts that are part of the common currency of our cultures. The

---

[52]   GS 17-18.

liturgy reminds us, as Christians, "we no longer live for ourselves but for him."[53] In this sense, our freedom is not something we achieve for ourselves, it is God's gift. To be really free to discern the times, the Church must always be conscious of the true nature and source of her freedom in history: freedom is the effect of grace that allows us to live for God and order our actions to His saving purpose. Our freedom is the most secure gift because it is God's own self-communication.[54] We possess it whatever the cultural or political circumstances of the age, whether we are accepted or persecuted, whether we can live openly or must be an "underground" Church. The Church lives in history with God's freedom. This is the constant witness of our history, at its most clear and intense in the witness of the martyrs, but always present in the resilience of faith in so many communities that have endured all attempts to erase them. The Church, therefore, is neither merely the product of history nor is it merely the victim of it, for in every age it is sustained by the Lord.

It may sound paradoxical, but the other aspect of this freedom is fidelity. The supreme demonstration of God's freedom is "taking flesh" in our time and history. It arises out of God's faithfulness - faithfulness to his own nature, so to speak: a God of love and mercy, the God who is faithful to his covenant, a God for us and with us. That faithfulness is the very essence of salvation. In history and through all its changes, God is faithful to Himself and His people. This Divine faithfulness is stated most clearly when the Risen Christ tells His Church that he will be with us to the end of time. The gift of the Spirit is already the fulfilment of that promise.

But it is not just a question of God's faithfulness to his community in history; it is also the community's

---

[53] Eucharistic Prayer IV.
[54] Gal.5:1.

118

faithfulness to what she has received from God - the revelation of His truth and mercy. The Church's fidelity is her obedience to this revelation, to the God who has made Himself known in history as Father, Son and Holy Spirit. Our secular culture has a great deal of trouble with the idea of "obedience", but you see here, in the life of faith, it is not an absence of freedom but its right ordering, so to speak; its alignment with the truth we have received and the goal that we seek, namely, God's will. It is like singing in tune or being so familiar with the instrument we play that we can improvise. Improvisation is not an abandonment of form but the bringing out of new capacities and potentials within it. Indeed, as we all know, sometimes the greatest spur to creative improvisation is being faced with limitation. But we cannot have the confidence to play or improvise creatively if we are afraid. The gift of freedom lived in this creative fidelity is a freedom from fear. It is remarkable how many times the Lord says to his disciples, "Be not afraid" or "Be not afraid, it is I." In Christ's presence, we are not afraid to face the truth. But if discerning the times is not to be an exercise in confirming our own prejudices, it must be based on an accurate knowledge about ourselves and the situations in which we live. This will come to us through many different channels, not just ecclesiastical ones. All of this used to be summed up in a popular formula you may recall – see, judge, and act.

The Signs of the Times: the *Kairos*

Another way of understanding this is in terms of finding the *kairos* - that moment when something of the power and energy of the Kingdom can be grasped and new possibilities realised - within the circumstances and movements of our age.

In the liturgy of Easter we celebrate that "all times belong to Him", and every age is inscribed within the "eternal now" of His resurrection. This is why we cannot evaluate "the times" in the way a secular atheist culture does. Nor can we adopt some grand philosophical or ideological view of history and its forces. It would be a distorted reading of history for us to look back to some "golden age" with nostalgia or to the future either with anxiety or a false utopian hope. Christ is present to us as Lord in every age for he is the "Alpha and Omega" present to us as our strength, our promise and our hope in every moment and place of our pilgrim journey. [55]

I think this is part of the key to *Gaudium et spes* and it is the source of our confidence in the face of all the difficulties and questions that inevitably face us. Our faith in the Risen Christ who is Lord of history is not a way of escaping history as critics might think. It is the way of living in it with a Christian freedom, realism, and moral vision that allows us to make each time, our time, a time of grace, because we know that it will always be filled with possibilities for transformation. In the beautiful words of Ps. 83, "Blessed are those whose strength is in you….. As they go through the dry valley, they make it a place of springs."[56]

I think this is one way of understanding what the Gospel means when it speaks of the *kairos* - God's time which is present in every time. Discerning the 'signs of the times' is seeking the *kairos* within them, the moment of new possibility, even when they are filled with darkness, confusion and death. It is from within the heart of these moments that the Church announces God's love and purpose for humanity:

"The Spirit of the Lord is upon me, because he has anointed me to preach the good news to the poor,

---

[55]   GS 45 echoing Heb. 13:8.
[56]   Taking the Latin version "dry valley" which is closer to the sense of the Hebrew

120

He has sent me to proclaim the release of captives and the recovering of sight to the blind, to set at liberty those who are oppressed and to proclaim the acceptable year of the Lord."[57]

Understood in this way, discerning the "signs of the times" is, in the deepest sense, an "evangelisation" - an announcing of the Gospel - as the new moment, the graced possibility for a transformed and redeemed society, lived in justice, peace, generosity and compassion.

For this reason the Church within culture and history always seeks to be a messenger of hope and friend of all women and men whatever their faith, race, status and situation, especially the poor and marginalized. True to *Gaudium et spes*, it does not pretend to have all the answers to every question. Yet, although it can look upon all the consequences of sin and its structures, it cannot despair; because of its faith in Christ it cannot lose faith in humanity.

Faced with the great weight of suffering and the histories of injustice and exploitation that mark our cultures, both national and international, the Church will always appear poor. Yet, like St. Peter in the Temple, it has the faith and the courage to say, "I have neither silver or gold, but I give you what I have; in the name of Jesus Christ of Nazareth, walk."[58] Now these are not just words, they come with the power of love that sees so many women and men give of themselves and their resources, risking their lives in the cause of justice, truth and peace that their sisters and bothers may "walk". This is why at the beginning of his pontificate, Pope Benedict stressed

---

[57]   Lk. 4:18-19; 2. Cor.6:1-11. Cf also Soc Rei. § 47.
[58]   Acts.3.6; 2. Cor. 4:7.

"that the Church is alive".[59]   It is alive because Jesus Christ is alive and present in his Church, and he offers the gift of life to the world.[60]   To discern the signs of the times is, then, to discern the way of the Gospel into the world - to follow the arc of the Incarnation - and by our ministry of patient love to make the *kairos* present as a graced possibility of transformation within every situation.

These reflections may seem a bit abstract, but we can see examples within the history of our own times. Even with all the historical qualifications that one would need to make, is it too much to see something of this *kairos* within the crisis that struck the papacy with the loss of the Papal States in the nineteenth century?   At the time, many thought that it was the end of the papacy as a significant power, but out of it came more clearly the spiritual and prophetic service of the papacy to the Church and humanity.   Again, out of the devastation of Europe after two world wars came the vision of Jean Monnet and Robert Schuman for a different sort of Europe.   Their aim was more than the creation of economic security, but real peace on a continent that had been torn by war and rivalry for too long.   They not only needed political skill but vision and stamina inspired by their faith to bring their dream to life.   Out of disaster, a new possibility, a new hope.   But this happens in more ordinary ways as well.   We see it in the lives of men and women like Jean Vanier and Charles de Foucauld, who keep a memory of the dignity and sacredness of all human beings whatever their status or

---

[59]   ".....the Church is alive. And the Church is young. She holds within herself the future of the world and therefore shows each of us the way towards the future. The Church is alive and we are seeing it: we are experiencing the joy that the Risen Lord promised his followers. The Church is alive – she is alive because Christ is alive, because he is truly risen." Homily, Mass. Imposition of the Pallium and conferral of the Fisherman's Ring. 25th April 2005.

[60]   Cf also Cons. Lit. Vatican II. § 7; esp. §33:"For in the liturgy God speaks to His people and Christ is still proclaiming His gospel. And the people reply to God both by song and prayer."

ability. Such people open up a sort of transcendence within the ordinary, and help us to value and reverence what we might dismiss or discard. In this way, they give us new possibilities for living and relating; they never allow us to devalue the currency of our lives for temporary gains. And, of course, all of us within our own experience will have experienced that moment of *kairos*. Often it will come when everything seems to have been lost or our plans have been completely upset. In these moments we have to rethink things, place them once again within the perspective of faith, come to a deeper sense of God's presence working in things. If we can do that we come to see that something else is open to us, maybe something we could not have seen before. Somewhere in the silence and the mess when all seems impossible the Angel announces to us, "Do not be afraid, for with God, nothing is impossible." In such moments we find ourselves in the *kairos*.

I have spent a little time on this important insight of *Gaudium et spes* because it helps us deepen our understanding of the way in which the Church is creatively present in our world. It helps us to see why there can be no wedge between the life of the Church and its mission. Our love of God cannot be separated from our love of neighbour and that is why to be a Christian is to be passionately committed to the building up of society and the shaping of our cultures; to the promotion of all that genuinely fosters the common good and enriches humanity.[61] It also enables us to see what is at the very heart of our activity and, therefore, the reason why we cannot accept the place allotted to us by a secularist version of society.[62] While respecting the autonomy of the political and civic spheres, our faith refuses to be content with a private room simply because the love of neighbour has to take us into the public sphere and, in the true spirit

---

[61] GS. 24; 36; Christifideles laici. § 42.
[62] GS.21.

of our Catholic vision, will always direct us to the neighbour who is beyond our borders. When we understand ourselves as called to open up within our times this *kairos* of Christ's presence, then we also use only the methods of Christ - the way of compassion and peace, the courage to speak the truth about our time but also to affirm and rejoice in its achievements for the common good, a commitment to reasoned, critical discourse with all constituencies and a moral vision which grasps that human dignity and freedom is first of all a theological reality, grounded in our vision of the value of every person made in the "image of God".[63] Our work is to heal and to reconcile, not wound and divide.[64] Above all, it is a vision of the fullness of human life, social and personal, a genuine solidarity or *communio*, which is not for these passing times only.[65]

Forty years on I think the Catholic Church, particularly the Church in England and Wales, has been shaped by *Gaudium et spes* and we can give thanks for what has been achieved. I also think that this is a new moment for us. So much is changing, but amidst the struggles and anxieties our society and culture is marked by a search for a new order of values and purpose. We can see it in a renewed sense of responsibility for the developing nations, the enormous generosity in the moments of international disasters, the commitment to the Make Poverty History campaign, the movements for international justice and peace that transcend party politics. We can see too, the growing commitment to human rights throughout the world not only at the level of international law but in the ethos and values of ordinary civic life. There is the growing awareness at every level of society that creation has to be respected and cherished

---

[63]   GS 17; 12. Cf. On The Participation of Catholics in Political Life. CDF. Doctrinal Note. 2003, esp §4; 5-6.
[64]   Matt. 42-44; GS § 28.
[65]   GS 25-26; Sol. Rei. Soc. § 39.

rather than ruthlessly exploited and instrumentalised. I also sense an new awakening to the issues of human life, from its beginning to its end, an awakening which became apparent to me, earlier this year, when I made a call for abortion to be an election issue, and found that I had touched a nerve among the British people, who are deeply worried about the number and lateness of abortions. These questions in particular go to the very heart of what constitutes an authentically humane, secure and civilised society. How we discuss them and how we legislate reveals the spiritual health or sickness of a culture.[66]

I think, too, we are beginning to rediscover the need for values that govern our public and social relations, for unless we can have trust and have confidence in our public institutions, the social good on which we rely for our private good is degraded. I was pleased that Mark Thompson was able to speak to the conference. I think we can and should be proud of our public service broadcasting, which is unique in the world. The Archbishop of Canterbury was correct in reminding us that the media have a vital role and responsibility for the creation of a positive culture of civic values.[67]

Although we can legislate to enshrine these values, law alone will never be sufficient to secure them. Here, I think, the Christian churches have played a significant part which needs to be acknowledged. The churches, through their support of family life, hospitals, schools, and an enormous range of charitable activities foster such public virtue. The Christian community continues to strengthen a social capital that has been depleted, partly due to the pressures of modernity, partly due to an

---

[66] Cf. discussion by Melanie Phillips, 'Heading for Extinction?' *Daily Mail*. June 22 2005.
[67] *The Media: Public Interest and Common Good*: lecture delivered at Lambeth Palace,Wednesday 15 June 2005

ideological denial of the social good of religion. It would be unfortunate for the common good if our society were to forget the richness that the Christian community brings to civic life and its commitment to fostering the public good.

These are some of the "signs of the times" - moments in which the *kairos* is present. Naturally, there are many challenges but no one should doubt that the Church is fully committed to the development of peoples and cultures.[68]

I believe we have an opportunity, and indeed an obligation, to engage in all the debates that are shaping our society. In doing so, I think we must always be conscious of two questions: How do we do this? Who do we reveal ourselves to be in doing it? Once again, I think that *Gaudium et spes* indicates our answers. Let me now turn to the first: How do we do this?

2. How to Engage our Culture: The Dialogue of Life

When we return to *Gaudium et spes*, we can see afresh the significance of its achievement. It describes an open and mutual relation between the Church and human society. Although the Church is not "the work of human hands" and its mission is not ultimately in the political, social or economic order, it freely acknowledges that it not only gives to human society but also receives from it.[69] This willingness to receive is critical for how we engage with contemporary society. It means that our relationship is one of genuine, creative dialogue and partnership. This is important. It would be too easy, faced with criticism and misunderstanding, to allow ourselves to be manoeuvred into a position of always seeming to be negative about our society. Our relationship is, of course, always a discerning one; it is not about acceptance, popularity, or

---

68   Pop. Prog.
69   GS 3; 42-45.

126

gain. That is the value of the freedom I spoke about earlier. Yet, it is not negative: "For God sent his son into the world, not to condemn the world" but that through him all may have eternal life.[70]

Now, how can the Church receive from society? *Gaudium et spes* sketches some of the things that we can recognise, but behind this lies a vision of God who is at work in all things. To put it in a more direct way, there are no "no-go" areas for God. And so we can discern even in the so-called "secular sphere" the work of His Spirit and the features of His Son. Let us call this the "dialogue of life", through which is disclosed "the depth of the riches of the wisdom and knowledge of God".[71]

The question of how we dialogue with this "world" is one that is always there for us. As the times and circumstances change, so we need to adapt to them. At times we will need to be more "a city on the Hill", clear, visible, confidently present. At other times we will need to emphasise more the hidden, but no less powerful, presence of being "the leaven in the dough". Again, it is not "either/or" but a matter of judgement about what is best for the situation in which we live and work. In most cases it will be both. *Gaudium et spes* does not provide us with a formula for this dialogue; it is a real dialogue not a series of interrupted monologues. Yet, I think the Constitution does provide us with orientations and dispositions. A good way of understanding this and entering into it is to take Christ's "dialogue of life" with the Samaritan woman at the well as our paradigm.

---

[70]   Jn. 3.16-18
[71]   Rom. 13:33

The Paradigm Dialogue: Jesus and the Samaritan Woman

The first thing that we notice is that Christ is on a journey and he comes in the ordinariness and need of his humanity. He is breaking the taboos in even associating with the woman, let alone asking her for a drink.[72] We meet the world in our common need. Like the Samaritan woman, we meet it not on the mountain or in some exalted academy but in the midst of the ordinary routines of life and life's struggles. The Samaritan woman first regards Christ as an "outsider", and so too secular society can regard us an "outsider". We have come to a place where we should not be, where we are not expected to be. We may be viewed with hostility, for secular society feels threatened: this is the territory it has claimed and defended as its own. Yet, we come to the well that is the world itself with all its goods.

You will remember that this well has a name, it is Jacob's well - the gift of the patriarch and common ancestor. The ancestor who carries the covenant of promise. The well marks a history. And here the meeting is already filled with meanings: a point where past and future converge, where history can turn to promise or disaster. Whenever we meet our culture we both come with the dust of the journey. So much division is rooted in history and the ways in which "history" is claimed. And like the woman at the well, we need to grapple with our histories, until we come to this point of convergence that is our common humanity, our frailty and longing. Then, from being strangers and antagonists we move beyond the roles we have been assigned and the burdens we carry to the beginning of an encounter - a real dialogue.

---

[72]   Cf. Barrett, C.K. *The Gospel according to St John : an introduction with commentary and notes on the Greek text.* London, SPCK. 1978. p.240.

The Gospel of John introduces its great motif of the journey. For John's Gospel is never just a matter of physical geography that has to be traversed, there is the sacred geography of the spirit; the journey from misunderstanding to understanding, from ignorance to truth, from death to life. It is not an easy one, for the woman has her truth, her identity and history but that patient, attentive, engagement of Christ who comes to her shows her how to come to him. It is a dialogue of respect, for without compromising his own truth, Christ never dismisses her truth.[73] Indeed, what unfolds for her is the deepest level of her own truth and longing - that from the beginning, whatever the circumstances of her life and culture, she has been seeking life, that life that only God can give, "Sir give me this water, that I may not thirst, nor come here again." Here, in her words, we have the deep desire of all human beings. Perhaps it is a desire that they are almost afraid to articulate; for who can answer it? And the Samaritan woman shows us, too, that it is never just a longing for material happiness, or spiritual consolation, it is a profound theological longing - a longing for God - and so, her response as the questions penetrate more deeply, "I know that the Messiah is coming, and when he comes, he will show us all things". [74]

We should never think that our dialogue with the world is just about the world; every search is a search for salvation however it expresses or describes itself. It is part of our service to humanity not only to enter into its search and longing, but also to be the memory, so to speak, of what that search is for. We have been entrusted with the truth that the search is never in vain or condemned to absurdity because, in Christ, God has met us at the well of our longing, He has searched for us and found us. In every age and at every well he meets us: "I who speak to you am he." In this moment, at Jacob's

---

[73]   GS 28
[74]   Jn.4:23. GS 41

well, the promise of the covenant is fulfilled and history is opened to a new future, a new history, and we begin a new journey, the journey of life.

In this dialogue the Church too, like the woman, comes to see the God who is forever *semper maior*. In and through this dialogue with the world, in obedience to its mission, the Church continues to receive the truth and enters into a deeper worship and praise: "You worship what you do not know; we worship what we know…but the hour is coming, and now is, when the true worshippers will worship the Father in spirit and truth, for such the Father seeks to worship him. God is Spirit, and those who worship him must worship him in spirit and in truth." In this way, the dialogue of life with the world becomes the dialogue of praise, an antiphon of Church and the world, nature and grace, which moves into doxology. And, as in the encounter with the woman at the well, Christ is no longer a stranger in a hostile land, but welcomed by those who were not his own, "So when the Samaritans came to him, they asked him to stay with them….' [75]   Like the woman, they discovered that they had lost nothing by taking him into their lives. Or, in the words of *Gaudium et spes,* "Whoever follows Christ, the perfect human being, becomes more of a human being."[76] Echoed recently by Pope Benedict, "If we let Christ into our lives, we lose nothing, nothing, absolutely nothing of what makes life free, beautiful and great."[77]

In the end, no dialogue or relationship will bear its fruit unless it is grounded in trust. And so *Gaudium et spes* calls on us to trust the world, or rather to trust God who is at work in His world. And it says to the world, you have nothing to fear from us, for the Church seeks only your good. Now, I do not think this is a naïve or idealised

---

[75]   Jn.4:40. NB.also the contrast with the Prologue: Jn.1:11. 'He came to his own home, and his own people received him not.'
[76]   GS 41
[77]   Inaugural Mass. Cf. Pop. Prog. §85.

relationship, we know that we are all on the pilgrimage of redemption, but, for the sake of Christ, we are committed to it.

3: Who are We in this Dialogue of Life? The Ecclesia Caritatis – the Church of Love

In the dialogue between Jesus and the Samaritan woman the question of identity is inevitable - Who are you? This is the second question I referred to earlier; it is a question the world constantly asks of us. It is asked with a variety of motives: with scepticism and cynicism, a benign indifference, a sort of puzzled query, for the Church doesn't fit any political or sociological type no matter how ingenious the analysis or nuanced the categories.

Who are you? Where do you come from? These are questions of identity which we also ask of ourselves as individuals and as a community, especially in times of transition and challenge. I think we are asking them today. They are symptoms of insecurity and loss of confidence. But it would be a mistake to think that that is all they are. They are also questions which reveal that we are alive, that we know that the mystery of our existence is still unfolding; they are questions that constantly take us back to the marvel of grace, to the God who has called us out of the darkness of nothingness into his own marvellous light. We cannot engage in the dialogue of life without the question of identity coming to the surface, for in that dialogue we disclose who we are. That can be painful. Too often we experience the discrepancy between our truth and our deeds. Our mistakes and weaknesses become evident as well as our goodness. But this, too, is part of our journey with the whole of humanity. We can acknowledge our weaknesses and mistakes with an honesty and humility before the world as the Holy Father, John Paul II did in preparation for the millennium in his great symbolic pilgrimage and acts of purifying the memory.

In the end, we should never be in any doubt about who we are and in whose image the Holy Spirit is forming us. That, too, can be read in the text of our history, but it is especially to be read in all the lives of simple holiness and love that constitute the reality of the Church. They are the living, practical experience of the truth we know theologically - namely, just as Christ reveals his identity in mission, so too does the Church. If, as I have been suggesting, *Gaudium et spes* is, in fact, a description of our mission in the world as the work of love, then love is our identity, we are an *ecclesia caritatis* – a church of love. This is the great theme of Vatican II as set out by Paul VI in opening the second session of the Council in 1963.[78] The Church cannot be anything less than this because she is established in the God who is love and she has received love as her new law from Christ, the love of God incarnate, "A new commandment I give to you, that you love one another; even as I have loved you. By this all will know that you are my disciples, if you have this love for one another."[79] This law is the source of the Church's unity and the reason why she seeks to promote unity, first among all Christian churches, and then among the whole human family. As St Thomas Aquinas expresses it, "The Church is one (...) through the unity of charity, because all are joined in the love of God, and among themselves in mutual love".[80]

Love of Neighbour and the Eucharist

Precisely because this love that we are and live is God's *self*-communication, it has within it a dynamism that

---

[78]   Cf. Speech, at the opening of the 2nd session of Vatican II 29 September 1963.
[79]   Jn.13:34-35. Cf. LG 9.
[80]   *Col* 3, 14. Thomas Aquinas, *Exposit. in Symbol. Apost.*, a. 9:

carries us always beyond ourselves to the whole of humanity – "*caritas Christi urget nos*" - the love of Christ impels us. [81] *Lumen gentium* says that the Church is the "sign and sacrament" and it is *Gaudium et spes* which shows us how this is a living sacrament of love that is real and practical. The true goal of all our planning and activity is to become, more and more, this *ecclesia caritatis* in the world. There is a form to this movement of loving service. To borrow an insight from Hans Urs Von Balthasar, it is a real "kenosis" or self-emptying which not only characterises the Church's inner life, but our life in the service of humanity as well.[82] This is why the Eucharist, the school of love and self-emptying at the heart of the Church, is never just a private act. It is the "the soul of the apostolate" from which all our acts of proceed.[83] That is why it is also the school of justice and peace. The memorial of Christ's passion is the table at which we daily sit with Christ's guests: the poor and the marginalized, the hungry, oppressed and homeless, the victims of war and tyranny. It is there that we meet them. It is from His table that we are sent forth in His name for them, to work practically and courageously, with every woman and man of good will, for the transformation of the structures that hold humanity in bondage and exploit the goods of creation.[84] This is a mission for every member of Christ's Body. As John Paul II reminded us in his message at the 14th World Youth Day in 1999, "Every situation of poverty is a challenge to each one's Christian charity. This charity, however, must become also social and political commitment, because the problem of poverty in the world depends on concrete situations that must be

---

[81]   2. Cor. 5:14.
[82]   Hans Urs Von Balthasar, *Explorations in Theology IV Spirit and Institution. The Kenosis of the Church*. pp.125-138. (ET by Edward. T Oakes SJ Ignatius Press, San Francisco. 1995).
[83]   LG 33;37. Apostolicam Actuositatem, 3ff, 6, 13, 15ff.
[84]   GS.24;38. LG.42.

changed by men and women of good will, builders of the civilization of love."[85]

And it is the first task of the Bishop to be a leader in this mission of love (*caritas pastoralis*), "coming to the help of the poor and the weak in every work of charity, whether they are members of the Church or not" [86] So, in a genuinely remarkable way, this love of the Church is free and disinterested. It is a free gift to the world and perhaps it can indicate a new way of living for our society, the leaven of the Kingdom that is hope for our culture and its institutions.

Conclusion

These are some reflections that I have wanted to share with you at the end of this Conference. You will be aware that my own motto is *Gaudium et spes*. My reason for living and hoping is simply the reality of God and his love for us manifest in the gift of His Son and the Holy Spirit. Like you, my reason for living is my hope of enjoying the vision of his Presence, and my deepest desire is to try to make this world a place in which all women and men can share that hope and experience God's love in their lives. That means that I am committed not only to an *ecclesia caritatis* but a "civilization of love".[87]

Perhaps St. Augustine has the best way of putting it, "so that by hearing the message of salvation the whole world may believe, by believing it may hope, and by hoping it may love."[88]

---

[85]   This was repeated again at the XV World Youth Day. It is a recurring theme in many of the writings and addresses of John Paul II.

[86]   LG. 27; 41. Christus dominus, 13;16.

[87]   Dives miser. 125.

[88]   Vatican II. De divine revelatione 1, citing Augustine, *De Cate. Rud.* 4, 8.